How to Say It with Your Voice

Applause for
How to Say It with Your Voice

In broadcast journalism, if you want a long and successful career you need *How to Say It with Your Voice*. In a practical systematic approach, this book teaches you exactly how to improve the most valuable tool you have for speaking with an audience—your voice.

DOW SMITH, ASSOCIATE PROFESSOR, BROADCAST JOURNALISM
S.I. Newhouse School of Public Communications, Syracuse University

Jeff's assistance has made a big difference in our presentation style during marketing presentations. We have won a lot more business since he began working with our firm. Everyone at Abbott feels he has helped us a great deal.

RAY HELD, PRESIDENT
Abbott Capital Management

Communicating is one of the most important things we do, and our voices are the vehicles through which we do this. Jeffrey Jacobi gives us the tools to improve the way we communicate. His methods will enrich your life.

STACEY TISDALE, TV CORRESPONDENT
CBS Market Watch

Well over one-third of your power to persuade depends directly on the sound of your voice. And Jeffrey Jacobi explains in rich, practical detail how to use yours to the best advantage. Read this book before the next time you have anything important to say.

JACK GRIFFIN
Author of How to Say It Best *and* How to Say It At Work

Packed with proven techniques and innovative strategies, *How to Say It with Your Voice* gives anyone who speaks on the job the practical tools to send a clear, confident and convincing message. Jeff provides the motivation and expertise to improve personal communication.

JAMES B. SGRITTO
Pediatric Health, Pfizer

If you want to impress others every time you speak, you want *How to Say It with Your Voice*. It's like having Jeff Jacobi as your personal voice trainer.

Whether you're hoping to stay on the top rung of the corporate ladder, or you're preparing to take your first step toward the executive suite, your voice can be one of your most valuable assets.

It can be your career's best friend.

JO BENNETT (EXECUTIVE SEARCH CONSULTANT), VICE PRESIDENT
Battalia Winston International

Jeff has helped me discover the right place in my voice to speak from. He has helped me find the key words that need to be emphasized with my voice, so that the audience can easily follow and understand the ideas. The better the delivery, the better the reception from the audience, and this in turn, has given me the confidence I need.

GAEL TOWEY
Creative Director, Martha Stewart Living Omnimedia

How to Say It with Your Voice is unique . . . offering the theory and practice required to polish and refine speech. Based on years of experience working with singers, actors, and business people . . . the author presents lively material . . . for anyone who needs to perform, manage others, appear in public, or deal with the local PTA.

CHRISTINE KELLY, ASSOCIATE PROFESSOR OF MANAGEMENT COMMUNICATION
Stern School of Business, New York University

It's not enough for professionals to have just a depth of knowledge and the ability to solve problems. They must also be able to communicate their thoughts with clarity and impact. Jacobi is right on the money with his insights and tips on developing a powerful and credible speaking ability.

CHARLES GOLDSMITH, PH.D.
Management Consultant to Financial Services Firms

Jeff Jacobi shares dozens of techniques for using your voice to exude greater presence, professionalism, personality, and power. Executives who want to enhance their leadership skills—or anyone who wants the world to take him or her more seriously—could benefit from this book.

DR. JUDITH B. ESTERQUEST, PRINCIPAL, SOE, INC.

It works! In a surprisingly simple, interesting and understanding manner, this book gave me the awareness and the tools to make an invaluable difference.

MARK SKLAR, VICE PRESIDENT
Remco Maintenance Corporation

Please don't think this book is just for professional speakers or actors. If you have a voice, you need this book. Jacobi takes technical information about the human voice and makes it easy to understand. This book is filled with practical advice that you will really use.

JOAN DETZ,
Author of How to Write and Give a Speech and Can You Say a Few Words?

How to Say It with Your Voice

Jeffrey Jacobi

Preface by William G. Parrett, Managing Partner, Deloitte & Touche LLP
Foreword by Tony Randall

Prentice
Hall Press

Library of Congress Cataloging-in-Publication Data

Jacobi, Jeffrey.
    The vocal advantage / Jeffrey Jacobi.
       p. cm.
    Includes index.
    ISBN 0-7352-0152-8 (pbk. w/CD) — ISBN 0-13-103664-5 (pbk. w/cassette)
    1. Public Speaking.   2. Voice culture.   I. Title.
PN4121.J23   1996
808.5'1—dc20   95–46008
                                                  CIP

Executive Editor: *Ellen Schneid Coleman*
Development Editor: *Sybil Grace*
Production Editor: *Jacqueline Roulette*
Formatting/Interior Design: *Robyn Beckerman*

©1996 by Prentice Hall, Inc.

CD ©2000 by Prentice Hall

Printed in the United States of America

10 9 8 7 6 5 4 3

ISBN 0-7352-0152-8 (pbk. w/CD)

This book is also published as *The Vocal Advantage.*

ISBN 0-13-103664-5 (pbk. w/cassette)

ATTENTION: CORPORATIONS AND SCHOOLS

Prentice Hall books are available at quantity discounts with bulk purchase for educational, business, or sales promotional use. For information, please write to: Prentice Hall Special Sales, 240 Frisch Court, Paramus, New Jersey 07652. Please supply: title of book, ISBN, quantity, how the book will be used, date needed.

 Paramus, NJ 07652

http://www.phdirect.com

In memory of my father, the late Henry Jacobi,
whose lifelong teachings were the inspiration for this book.

Acknowledgments

My heartfelt thanks to my mother, Tanya, and to my wife, Rosemary, for their continuous support and encouragement, and to my son, Michael, with love and affection.

Special thanks to Ellen Schneid Coleman, Sybil Grace, Jeff McCartney, Suzette Haden Elgin, and Sanford Teller for their help and guidance.

About the Author

Jeffrey Jacobi is a nationally renowned speech coach and Owner and Director of Jacobi Voice Development in New York City. He has worked with executives from the cream of Fortune 500 companies, including AT&T, American Express, DuPont, Merrill Lynch, Nabisco, as well as entertainers and the media. He is the author of *The Executive Voice Trainer* (Prentice Hall), and has taught speech communication at New York University.

Contents

Part 1
Identifying Speech Problems
You Want to Solve / 9

Part 2

Building Your Vocal Advantage / 131

Part 3

Using Your New Vocal Advantage to Reach Your Goals / 191

9 *Overcoming the Fear of Public Speaking to Sound Confident and Poised.* *221*

Preface

I'm not sure exactly when I began to think about how effective I was as a speaker. It was probably at a point when growing responsibilities required me to talk to increasingly larger audiences. Until then my communications with clients, associates and others had been in more intimate settings, such as board meetings, client conferences, and small group business meetings. Communication was informal, consisting of questions, opinions, directions and listening. Vigorous give and take provided the time and opportunity to clarify one's point of view.

When I began to speak to larger audiences of 75, 500, or 2000 it was obviously important to begin with a well-prepared, organized talk on a meaningful subject about which I was knowledgeable and felt strongly. But, there was more to it. I began to notice, that because the audience could not respond to, or question my comments, at least until the end of my talk, they were observing me more closely, not only on what I said, but on how I sounded and looked.

Through feedback and taped recordings I began to get a better idea of how I sounded and looked to my audience. There were both good and bad revelations, but there was no question that I wanted to perform at a higher level. This was reinforced when I began to observe other speakers more closely, some wonderfully dynamic and effective.

As I have done at other times in my career, when I've wanted to improve at something, I sought expert help. That is how I met Jeff Jacobi, who has worked with many of the Fortune 500 top executives. Personal coaching from Jeff and reading his book have introduced me to various strategies for capturing and holding the favorable attention of an audience. I've learned the importance of pausing between phrases, changing the pitch and pace of my voice, and emphasizing the right words for impact. Avoiding clichés and the overuse of idioms (for which my international partners are grateful) and moderating my New York style (for which my southern partners are equally grateful) have helped me better relate to my audience. Perhaps, most important, I've become aware of my own unique talents and how to make the most of them. This has given me greater confidence to express myself naturally, with authority and conviction, in any speaking situation.

The act of improvement can tend to lead one to further raise one's standards and expectations of performance. That's the way this speaking thing seems to work. There's always another level to reach.

If what I've said here strikes a responsive chord I believe this book will give you the foundation and impetus to become the effective and dynamic speaker you want to be. It's your call.

William G. Parrett
Managing Partner, Deloitte & Touche LLP

Foreword

When I was about fifteen I decided to become an actor and badgered my parents until they let me study. My teacher drilled me in articulation. I was lucky in having few really bad faults. My teacher had a deep, beautiful voice. Naturally, I imitated him. Soon people began telling me that I had a beautiful voice. I went to college and majored in speech. Every morning for a year we had an hour's drill in consonants and vowels. We learned how to pronounce frequently mispronounced words. We made records at the beginning and end of the term. I could hear that my speech had improved. Both teachers and students admired my voice, to which by then I had added a tremolo copied from an actor I admired. Later, I went to drama school where I received two more years of excellent speech training. Upon graduation I was offered a position teaching voice and speech. Everyone considered me an authority, especially my pupils.

Throughout, I had been doing a great deal of acting, of course. This, the real test of my voice, gave me plenty to worry about. I knew that, because my articulation was clean and well tutored, I could be understood. People liked my voice because it had a naturally pleasant quality and it sounded deep. It was my secret that I forced it to be deep. However, if I spoke that way in a large auditorium, I couldn't be heard. Furthermore, when I raised my voice it no longer sounded good; it lost its quality. If the scene demanded power, I could only yell; I could not raise my voice without it becoming raucous and strained. After a performance, I frequently had a sore throat. I had no idea what to do about it, and I stubbornly believed that I had a well-trained voice and that I knew a lot about the subject.

About this time I spent a summer in the theater with an actor whose primary interest was singing. His voice amazed me. It had a boom and ring to it that I could not duplicate no matter how hard I tried to imitate him. On stage with him I had to shout to equal his normal vocal level. In big scenes he could roar like a bull without effort and without fatigue and without losing his mellifluous quality. Even choked up with a cold he had more voice than I had at my best.

It was then that I asked myself, how could I attain such power and freedom and quality? I think my development began with that question. In time my search led me to the approach laid forth in this book. The rest is history.

For most of you, who are not actors, I can hear you asking another question.

What you say makes sense for actors, but why do other professionals such as doctors, lawyers, teachers and business people need to think about how they use their voices? The answer is really quite simple. Your voice is your key communication tool. It literally speaks volumes about who you are and determines how the world hears and sees you. The way you speak is often more important to how people first judge you than your experience, intelligence, education, appearance—or personality. In short, how you use your voice can help you or hurt you. It can win or lose a big sale. It can inspire confidence and assurance. *Or* it can generate doubt and anxiety.

The good news is that you can change the way you sound. In this innovative book, Jeffrey Jacobi shows you how to overcome common speaking problems you may have while building on the natural qualities and strengths of your own voice. It's a simple but proven approach to voice development that's effective, easy to learn and richly rewarding.

Tony Randall

How This Book Will Help You

When you decided to buy *How to Say It with Your Voice*, you made it clear that you aren't like most people. This book will show you how to train your voice to create a positive impression, maximize overall performance, and generate a strong and competitive business edge. It uses a simple but proven approach that builds on the natural qualities of your own voice. You'll learn how to use those qualities to their fullest to achieve the best possible results.

- Do you have difficulty projecting your voice in a large room?
- Do people often ask you to repeat what you have said?
- Do you have a hard time keeping your listeners' attention?
- Do people seem to have difficulty understanding your speech?
- Do you feel you have been passed over for promotion because of your voice or speech?

With the help of the self-testing techniques offered in this text, you will be able to identify your vocal problems readily. When you have completed the program, you'll fully understand the voice problems you may have—and you'll know exactly how to solve them.

The approach presented in this book consists of a series of exercises that will:

- Strengthen and polish your voice and delivery to give you power and confidence in any situation.
- Transform the impression you make on others when you speak so you can effectively communicate your ideas.

Practice words, phrases, and sentences sections, as well as longer reading selections, will help you easily master each new skill. In fact, using the 12-Minute Vocal Workout is enough to produce dramatic results.

With *How to Say It with Your Voice*, you'll:

- Avoid sounding nasal or whiny;
- Pronounce words clearly so you will always be understood;
- Modify the pitch of your voice so people will be able to concentrate on your message, not on your voice quality;
- Overcome any fear of speaking in public.

In addition, brief scenarios based on real-life experiences demonstrate the range of vocal and speech problems this book will help you solve.

Don't let your competitors have the edge. Join the many businesspeople who have achieved the vocal advantage:

- The corporate executive who overcame a soft, monotonous voice and regional accent to give successful presentations
- The lawyer who strengthened his weak voice to gain success in winning courtroom arguments
- The senior account executive (whose high-pitched voice once set off a key-chain car alarm), who lowered the pitch of his voice to gain vocal resonance and strength—and credibility
- The assistant vice president (whose thin soft voice made it hard for her to make herself understood), who gained the confidence and power to make a successful presentation to a roomful of people, none of whom asked her to speak louder because they couldn't hear her

Gain the vocal advantage and keep it for yourself. Boost your own performance and give your own natural abilities and knowledge the best possible chance for success, with *How to Say It with Your Voice*. Let's begin.

1

Improve Your Business Voice: It's the Best Investment You'll Ever Make

HOW A SOFT, BREATHY VOICE CAN LOSE A DEAL

"And so," Marian Ellerbee said, closing the folder that held her notes, "I'm confident that you will agree with our proposal. Just tell me when you'd like to start the new campaign and we'll get it underway for you!"

Marian *did* feel confident. The proposal was one of the best her agency had ever come up with. And she had done her homework. She'd had an answer ready for every question the clients had raised; she'd had every fact and statistic right on the tip of her tongue. They'd go for the campaign; she was *sure* of it!

But then, as she paused just outside the conference room door to put her papers into her briefcase, she was stunned by what she heard them saying behind her . . .

"Maybe they have some good ideas, but they obviously don't feel any enthusiasm for our new product at all!"

"I know what you mean . . . Ellerbee knew all the facts, sure, but you could tell—she was just going through the motions."

What Went Wrong Here? All the hard work this advertising account executive had done to offer her client an irresistible proposal was wasted—because her soft, breathy voice made her presentation sound weak and lackluster. She was enthusiastic about the client's product and about the fine campaign her staff had created. But that didn't come through to the people listening to her—and she didn't get the account.

HOW RAPID-FIRE SPEECH DOESN'T GET THE ORDER

"Well? Whaddaya say? Y'ready t'go ahead on this?" Jack Nelson grinned and slapped an order blank down on the desk, pen at the ready. "How many units, Fred? Three? Five? How about five t'start with?"

Fred Whittier cleared his throat and stared down at his desk, trying to keep his voice pleasant in spite of the way he felt. He said only, "I'll have to get back to you later, Jack. I'm not ready to make a decision right now." But what he was thinking was a lot less polite: *"I wouldn't buy from you, buddy, if you were the last supplier in the state!"*

He showed the sales representative out, glad to see the last of him. When the door had closed behind the other man, Fred turned to his assistant and said, "You know what he reminds me of? Those guys at the carnivals. The ones who always tell you you'll win the giant teddy bear, but you never win anything but one of those crummy paper fans!"

"He's a fast talker, all right," she agreed.

"He sure is—he's so fast he talked himself right out of an order," Fred said. "I didn't trust him for one minute!"

What went wrong? It's obvious. Jack Nelson may be a skilled salesman. He may be selling a fine product. But that's not going to be enough—not when his rapid-fire speech makes customers feel uneasy and distrustful. He won't be getting an order from Fred Whittier. Not now; not later.

HOW THE WAY YOU TALK CAN UNDERMINE YOUR PROMOTION PROSPECTS

When good ol' boy Sam came charging through the front door, his wife knew instantly that he hadn't gotten the promotion. He was so furious, smoke was practically coming out of his ears.

"Honey . . ." Evelyn began; she meant to tell him that there'd be plenty of other opportunities and that he shouldn't let this one setback get to him. But he cut her off.

"You know why they didn't give me that fool promotion?" he shouted at her. "*I'll* tell you why! Because the way I talk doesn't happen to suit their high-falutin majesties, *that's* why! I'm just *way* too down home for them, Evvie! Never mind I'm the best man they've got in this division! Never mind I've been here five years longer than the twit they passed me over for! Never mind how good my work is or how loyal I am or anything else along *those* lines! The only thing that matters to them is their bleeping image! It makes me so mad I could *spit*!"

Evelyn bit her lip and tried to think of something comforting to say. It wasn't going to be easy; it wasn't the first time they'd done this to him. And it wasn't *fair.*

Being Judged by Your Speech Can Put You at a Vocal Disadvantage

Certainly, it's not fair. It's not fair for Marian Ellerbee's otherwise excellent presentation and hard work to go down the drain—just because she sounds like a bored child when she talks. It's not fair for Jack Nelson to lose a sale—just because his delivery makes customers think of con men they've encountered in the past. It's not fair for a top employee like Sam Lewis to be passed over for promotion for someone a lot less capable and valuable than he is—just because the company is afraid that people will be turned off by his hillbilly accent. None of that is fair. Good work and solid value *ought* to be enough!

However, this is the real world, which isn't always a fair place. And it's simply a fact of life that many business professionals have the talent and motivation to move ahead, but common problems with the way their voices sound—and the way they *use* their voices—hold them back and become barriers to their success. When a politician's hoarseness during a key campaign speech means that only people in the front rows are able to hear him . . . when an international consultant's foreign accent makes her words difficult to understand . . . when a store owner's shrill high-pitched voice annoys customers so much that they go elsewhere, even at higher prices . . . when a lawyer's arguments are shot down again and again by someone on the other side who has not more powerful arguments but a more powerful speaking voice and manner . . . *none* of that is fair.

But like it or not, in these situations and hundreds more of the same kind, people are judged not by what they know or do, and not by the content of their speech, but simply *by the way they sound* to others. According to a recent study, nearly forty percent of the first impression you make on other people is based entirely on the sound of your voice. Just think what this can mean to you during the opening moments of a job interview or a sales pitch!

Research proving that the most critical parts of human interaction depend primarily on the sound of the voice and the way the voice is used has been around for many many years. Nothing you can do for your image will give you as much bang for the buck as improving the way you *sound* will; nothing can do you more damage, more unjustly, than a *negative response* to the way you sound. We all know that; it's not news. But most of us spend our money and energy on the way we *look*—on expensive clothes and haircuts and watches and desks—without devoting any of our resources to that single, and far more important problem. According to Annalyn Swan ("On Speaking Terms," *Allure*, April 1995) vocal professionals agree that "One of the chief reasons for the sloppy, inelegant, and whiny way we now speak . . . is that we are so obsessed with appearance that we can't see beyond the ends of our noses."

Identifying Your Vocal Potential

The first step is to get a good idea of how your voice sounds to others *right now*, so that you'll have a baseline against which to measure your progress. To do that you'll need to make a tape of your own speech.

You don't have to have fancy equipment. Today's ordinary inexpensive cassette recorders are fully capable of giving you an accurate tape that sounds the same way to you as you sound to others. You need to record about twenty minutes of your speaking voice, while you talk about something that interests you. Don't read aloud or try to make a speech; just talk naturally about something that you care about and is familiar to you. (The most valuable teacher you ever had, for example, or your favorite restaurant, how you feel about Congress, and so on.) Talk for long enough to get over feeling self-conscious and to provide yourself with an adequate sample.

And then, *listen carefully* to your tape, all the way through, and answer the questions that follow as honestly and completely as you can. (If you don't feel confident about answering a particular question, ask someone else to listen and help you make the necessary judgments.)

WHAT TO LISTEN FOR WHEN YOU HEAR YOURSELF ON TAPE

1. Is your voice high-pitched?

2. Is your voice too loud or too soft?

3. Do you talk too fast—or too slowly?

4. Do you sound nasal—as if you're talking through your nose?

5. If you had to describe your voice to someone else, would you use any of the following words?

   shrill   raspy   squeaky   rough   whiny   monotonous

6. Do you say your words clearly, making them easy to understand?

7. Are your words complete? (For example, do you drop your "g's" and say "goin'" for "going"? Do you cut off the ends of words and say "lef" for "left"?)

8. Do you salt your speech with fillers like "you know" and "okay" and "uh . . ."?

9. Do you frequently clear your throat or make other noises that interrupt your speech?

10. Do you sound confident or uneasy?

11. Do you sound interested or bored?

12. Does your voice trail off at the end of sentences?

13. Do you sound like someone with authority?

14. When you make a statement does it sound like you're asking a question?

15. Imagine that you are someone else. Would you enjoy listening to the person on the tape?

REVIEWING YOUR PREVIOUS VOCAL EXPERIENCE

Answer the following questions to help you complete your vocal profile.

1. When you talk, do people frequently ask you to repeat yourself?

2. Is it an effort for you to project your voice in a large room?

3. Do you frequently finish talking sooner than you intended—or do you frequently run out of time?

4. Do people tell you that you have an accent?

5. Do others frequently interrupt you or talk over you?

6. Does your voice ever quiver when you're nervous?

7. Do you get hoarse after you've talked a while?

8. Do you have a hard time getting and keeping your listeners' attention?

9. Do you *worry* about how you'll sound before you begin a meeting or presentation?

10. Do other people seem to enjoy talking with you and hearing you talk to them—or do you have a feeling that they try to avoid those experiences?

Now you have your baseline information. Write the day on the tape and on the answers to the questions, and put them away for safekeeping. You'll want to compare them with new tapes and answers later, as your voice begins to change and improve.

How to Practice to Gain the Vocal Advantage

As you practice the voice and speech improvement exercises in this book, remember to start out slowly. This gives your muscles a chance to get the "feel" of the exercises. It also provides the necessary time to make sure you are doing the exercises correctly. Once you master each exercise at a slow tempo, gradually build up speed until you reach your normal rate of speech. You may need to repeat a particular exercise five, ten or even fifteen times at graduated speeds to ensure that the improvements you want to make become ingrained in your speech. This may require a bit more of your time, but it's the only way to get good results and eliminate the "hit or miss" syndrome that often results from fast and sloppy practicing.

Whenever possible, try to finish a drill or exercise using a conversational tone. Many students are able to perform an exercise well, yet when they finish practicing and resume their normal speech patterns, many of the old habits creep back in again. Ending an exercise with a conversational tone helps bridge the gap between exercise and reality and allows your new improved skills to become an integral part of your everyday speech. Remember, changing old habits takes time so start out slowly and deliberately and be patient.

Part 1

Identifying
Speech Problems
You Want to Solve

2
Getting Rid of "Sloppy" Speech to Improve Communication

HOW "SLOPPY" SPEECH CAN HOLD YOU BACK

Wade Smith had been waiting for today's performance review for months. He knew he had been doing well: His sales figures had been going up steadily; he'd brought in more than a dozen new accounts this year; he got along well with his colleagues. Also, two of his ideas for cutting costs were under consideration by the company. Knowing all this, he was relaxed when he sat down across the desk from his supervisor Jerry Ramirez; he expected some constructive criticism, but he was sure the review would be positive overall.

What he heard wasn't what he was expecting, however. It started out all right, but it went downhill in a hurry.

"Wade," Jerry said, "I want you to know that everybody here is pleased with your work and appreciates the efforts you make to do a good job. Your numbers are pretty impressive."

"Thanks, Jerry. It's good to hear you say that."

"However . . ." Jerry paused for a minute, and then said, "However, I have to tell you that in spite of all the credit you're entitled to, we can't offer you a promotion at this time."

"But the company's profits are way up," Wade said, puzzled. "I don't understand."

"The problem's not with company profits," Jerry said. "The problem is with you."

"I don't understand," Wade said again. "I thought you said I was doing really well."

"You are. But you can't qualify for a promotion with this company until you do something about your sloppy speech. Wade, I have to be brutally honest: We can't have you talking to clients and the public sounding the way you do."

"I don't know what you mean," Wade told him. "What's the *matter* with the way I talk?"

Jerry shook his head. "I'm no communications expert, Wade; I'm not equipped to explain it to you. But if I were you, I'd make a tape of myself talking, and I'd listen to it the way I'd listen to the most important speech I ever heard. I think you'll be genuinely surprised at how you sound."

Jerry was right. At first, as Wade listened to the tape he'd made, it seemed to him that he sounded just like anybody else. But he knew Jerry too well to think that there wasn't something there to hear, and he made an effort to listen to it as if he were hearing someone else talking instead of listening to himself. And when he really concentrated on the speech on tape, he had to admit it: he wouldn't be easy for people to understand. He sounded like somebody talking with a mouthful of marbles! It was depressing and embarrassing, but it was clear to Wade that the evaluation had been fair. It was also clear that he wasn't going to get ahead at this company—maybe not at *any* company—until he found a way to improve his speech.

And he realized that even though Jerry's words had hurt, the man had actually done him a favor. This was something he really needed to know about, and really needed to *fix*. If only somebody had brought it to his attention a long time ago!

Defining "Sloppy" Speech

When Jerry calls Wade's speech "sloppy," he's using a term with no scientific value; as he said himself, he's not a communications expert.

But "sloppy" speech (sometimes called "lazy speech" or "lazy tongue") is a term in common use to describe what many people perceive as the speech of a person who just can't be bothered to pronounce words clearly and completely.

They're incorrect. All the varieties of English that tend to be given this label are just as systematic and require just as much physical and mental effort as any other. The problem is that people whose dialects are closer to "Standard English"—like Jerry—don't realize that what they're hearing is just what happens when someone uses various non-standard rules. It's not laziness that causes speakers to drop the "l" sound in "help" or the "r" sound at the end of "car." It's the fact that in their dialects, the rules of the sound system require them to do precisely those things.

However, you're not likely to spend much of your business day talking to people who are communications experts. This means that if your way of talking is nonstandard, people listening to you will probably think your speech is sloppy or lazy. The impression they get will be negative, and they will tend to assume that if you are "sloppy" and "lazy" in your speech, you are sloppy and lazy in other ways as well. Your own speech is not wrong, but your chances of making a good impression on others will be far greater if you make a few changes.

How to Find Out If You Have a "Sloppy" Speech Problem

To find out if you, like Wade, are being held back by this problem, analyze your pronunciation of the items in the list that follows. Say the words the way you would ordinarily pronounce them, without making any extra effort. Pay very close attention to the sounds you hear yourself make, to find out whether or not you pronounce as many sounds as are shown in parentheses right after each word. For example, you'll see "can't" and then the number (4); this means that when Standard English speakers say "can't" they pronounce four distinct sounds. How many sounds do you hear when you say "can't"?

Also, notice the sounds shown in italics. These are frequently omitted by sloppy speakers. For example, you'll see that "can't" has the "n" and "t" in italics. This indicates that Standard English speakers pronounce the final "nt" sound. Do you hear the final "nt" sound when you say "can't"?

Taping the list and listening to your tape is the best way to proceed, but you may be able to check your pronunciation just by speaking aloud and listening carefully.

"SLOPPY" SPEECH TEST LIST

ca*n't* (4)	we*nt* (4)	dista*nt* (7)	se*nd* (4)
frie*nd* (5)	mi*dst* (5)	bes*t* (4)	des*k* (4)
reco*g*nize (7)	tes*ts* (5)	hope*d* (4)	sal*t* (4)
wi*ld* (4)	dra*ft* (5)	stric*t* (6)	ke*pt* (4)
pa*rk* (4)	doo*r* (3)	la*rg*e (4)	wi*dth* (4)

This list is not complete, but it covers many of the problem areas. If you found that you weren't pronouncing the sounds written in italics, your speech may well be the kind that people call "sloppy." The drills and exercises that follow will help you correct the problem and learn to use a more standard pronunciation.

How to Solve Your "Sloppy" Speech Problems

When you first start practicing, you'll want to slightly exaggerate your pronunciation to give your muscles a chance to train themselves to follow the new rules. This is only a temporary strategy, however. Obviously, if you "o-ver-e-nun-ci-ate" you run the risk of going too far in the opposite direction from sloppy to sounding phony. While your goal is to achieve clear and distinct pronunciation, you should always try for a natural and easy delivery. Remember: *good speech should never call attention to itself.*

DON'T DROP THOSE FINAL CONSONANTS!

Dropping final consonants is one of the most common enunciation problems, for many native-born speakers as well as foreigners. Final consonants are often dropped when they follow other consonants. For example, the word "wa*nt*" may come out sounding like "wan" or the word "so*ld*" may sound like "sole." The following section reviews some of the most troublesome final consonant combinations and tells you how to deal with them.

Practicing the Final "NT" Sound

PRACTICE EXERCISE: TENT.   To make a clean "t" sound, the tip of your tongue has to hit the roof of your mouth. Hold your hand right in front of your mouth. Start by saying the word "*te*n." Feel the tongue position on the initial "t" sound. Now add the final "t" and say "ten*t*." Make sure you release the tongue tip on the final "t" sound. If you are doing this right, you will feel a little puff of air on the back of your hand after each "t" sound.
Repeat the word "ten*t*."

PRACTICE WORDS AND SENTENCES.   Pronounce each word ending carefully.

can't	rent	account	event
point	payment	frequent	intent
went	amount	constant	patent
comment	instant	consent	recent
moment	absent	tenant	segment
client	vacant	percent	couldn't
discount	present	placement	implement
statement	shipment	didn't	component
urgent	shouldn't	accountant	continent
wouldn't	competent	investment	meant
efficient	different	count	want
resistant	won't	spent	
don't	sent	appoint	

My client is at the event.

The president was absent.

We need to supplement the investment.

His statement was significant.

Don't make an appointment.

The apartment is vacant.

At present, I have no comment.

Practicing the Final "ND" Sound

PRACTICE EXERCISE.   To pronounce the final "d" sound clearly, you have to let your tongue tip hit the roof of the mouth and make sure you release it. There isn't any one syllable English word that starts with "d" and ends with "nd," but let's pretend there is one—let's practice with the invented word "dend." Put your hand right in front of your mouth. Say "d," paying close attention to the position of your tongue. Say "den"; now add a final "d" for "dend." As happened when you practiced the real word "tent," if you're doing it right you will feel a little puff of air on the back of your hand after each "d" sound.

You'll be wondering why, since you do exactly the same thing for both "t" and "d," you get two different sounds. It's because the only difference between the two is that "d" is *voiced* and "t" is *unvoiced*. When you say a voiced sound, your vocal cords vibrate; when you say an unvoiced sound, they don't. There's an easy way to make this absolutely clear. Just follow these steps:

1. Put your fingertips against the front of your throat.

2. Now make a long "zzzzzzzzzzzzzzz" sound, like a bee buzzing. Feel the vibration against your fingertips? That's because you're voicing the sound.

3. Now make a long "sssssssssssss" sound, like a snake hissing. Notice—you don't feel any vibration against your fingertips. That's because you're not voicing the sound.

PRACTICE WORDS AND SENTENCES

send	comprehend	profound	remind
amend	tend	find	fund
thousand	understand	correspond	shorthand
extend	command	underground	rebound
dividend	beforehand	grand	land
attend	bend	blind	blend
errand	expand	almond	end
demand	fond	and	behind
pretend	sand	defend	round
found	refund	intend	blond
second	recommend	beyond	
mind	hand	respond	

We'll pretend to understand.

I demand a refund.

He's second in command.

They must expand the land.

Give me a hand at the end.

Let's correspond in shorthand.

Never mind, just find the dividend.

PRACTICING OTHER FINAL CONSONANT COMBINATIONS

The Final "LT" Sound

PRACTICE EXERCISE: SALT.   Follow these three steps:

1. Say "saw."

2. Say "saw-l-t." Feel your tongue tip touching the roof of your mouth on the "l" sound, then release the tongue tip on the final "t" sound.

3. Say "salt."

PRACTICE WORDS AND SENTENCES.   Use the same procedure for the following:

insult	difficult	dealt
melt	halt	consult
result	built	belt
guilt	adult	vault
tilt	Roosevelt	default
fault	lilt	

That wasn't too difficult.

All the money is in the vault.

Please pass the salt.

As a result, it was never built.

According to the adult, this was not his fault.

The Final "LD" Sound

PRACTICE EXERCISE: OLD.   Follow these three steps:

1. Say "owe."
2. Say "owe-l-d." Feel the tip of your tongue touching the roof of your mouth on the "l" sound, then release the tongue tip on the final "d" sound.
3. Say "old."

PRACTICE WORDS AND SENTENCES.   Use the same procedure for the following:

bold	sold	windshield
fold	Donald	cold
mold	withhold	hold
yield	child	world
withheld	held	upheld
build	told	field
guild	threshold	mild

She held out for a better yield.

They can't build in the field.

Donald has a cold.

We told them it was sold.

The Final "FT" Sound

PRACTICE EXERCISE: DRAFT.　Follow these three steps:

1. Say "dra."
2. Say "dra-f-t."
3. Say "draft."

PRACTICE WORDS AND SENTENCES.　Use the same procedure for the following:

craft	raft	thrift
theft	makeshift	adrift
shift	spacecraft	sift
uplift	left	loft
handcraft	soft	swift
drift	aircraft	gift
shaft	lift	

I need a lift.

The gift was in the loft.

At the light, make a left.

This is only a rough draft.

The Final "CT" Sound

PRACTICE EXERCISE: FACT.   Follow these three steps:

1. Say "fa."
2. Say "fa-k-t." Keep in mind that the final "ct" spelling is actually pronounced "kt."
3. Say "fact."

PRACTICE WORDS AND SENTENCES.   Use the same procedure for the following:

strict	act	expect	indirect
contract	effect	aspect	correct
impact	object	instinct	dialect
product	architect	contact	prospect
compact	eject	react	adjunct
afflict	attract	collect	conduct
conflict	connect	distract	elect
enact	instruct	subject	perfect
predict	protect	reject	restrict
select	retract	subcontract	

Please select a new product.

In fact, we have no contract.

His dialect made an impact.

I can't predict how they'll react.

In effect, this may conflict.

The Final "PT" Sound

PRACTICE EXERCISE: TEMPT.   Follow these three steps:

1. Say "tem."
2. Say "tem-p-t."
3. Say "tempt."

PRACTICE WORDS AND SENTENCES.   Use the same procedure for the following:

crept	kept	prompt	adept
slept	wept	abrupt	concept
adopt	attempt	adapt	erupt
disrupt	bankrupt	contempt	preempt
Egypt	except	exempt	script
intercept	unkempt	accept	corrupt

The organization was tax exempt.

Make an attempt to understand the concept.

We accept only one script.

In Egypt, they went bankrupt.

The Final "ST" Sound

PRACTICE EXERCISE: LOST.   Follow these three steps:

1. Say "law."
2. Say "law-s-t."
3. Say "lost."

PRACTICE WORDS AND SENTENCES.   Use the same procedure for the following:

best	contrast	overcast
last	exist	economist
must	invest	west
vast	request	test
assist	utmost	almost
contest	optimist	consist
enlist	therapist	digest
insist	east	honest
protest	midst	nearest
tourist	rest	suggest
interest	against	analyst
specialist	broadcast	pessimist
cost	dentist	violinist
list	forecast	just
past	longest	most
adjust	resist	toast
August	typist	

This is only a test.

I insist that she's honest.

We lost the list.

I propose a toast.

What will the rest of this cost?

We'll invest in August.

She's in the midst of the contest.

They suggest you see a dentist.

What's the latest request?

Final "STS"

Many speakers make the mistake of dropping the "ts" in "sts" endings. For example, "lists" often comes out sounding like "liss." To get the right pronunciation practice the word in three steps:

1. Stop on the first "s" of the "sts" ending and say: "liss."
2. Add the "t" sound, then "s," and say "liss-t-s."
3. Join "liss" and "t-s" together without stopping the sound and say: "lists."

PRACTICE WORDS AND SENTENCES.   Use the same procedure for the following:

costs	contests	suggests
lasts	contrasts	tourists
rests	digests	typists
arrests	exists	analysts
tests	forecasts	interests
hosts	dentists	specialists
toasts	insists	therapists
adjusts	invests	economists
assists	protests	geologists
broadcasts	requests	pianists
consists	resists	violinists

The illness resists all medication.

Please answer the requests.

This lasts a long time.

That costs too much.

There were many economists at the meeting.

PRACTICE WORDS AND SENTENCES, cont'd.

The tourists have the lists.

The hosts made all the toasts.

She insists the tests are fair.

MASTERING THE "SK" SOUND

There's one word of English that people give such importance to in judging other speakers, which is completely out of proportion: the word "ask." It's just one word, but because the impression made by its nonstandard pronunciation is so negative, we'll give it its own section here. In some varieties of English, people pronounce "ask" exactly the way they pronounce "axe." It seems trivial, but it's like the word "ain't"—it creates an instant bad impression.

The simplest way to fix this is to say the word "mask." Then take away the "m" and say "ask." Make sure you pronounce the final "k" sound clearly.

PRACTICE WORDS AND SENTENCES

brisk	whisk	frisk
mask	picturesque	grotesque
task	bask	dusk
asterisk	tusk	risk
desk	husk	
flask	disk	

Ask for the axe.

Give Max the mask.

The task was to prepare the tax.

The disk is on the desk.

We'll help you manage the risk.

Final "SKS"

Some speakers make the mistake of dropping the final "ks" for "sks" endings. For example, "disks" often sounds like "diss." For the right pronunciation, practice the word in these three steps:

1. Stop on the first "s" of the "sks" ending and say: "diss."
2. Add the "k" sound, then the "s" sound, and say: "diss-k-s."
3. Join "diss" and "k-s" together without stopping the sound and say: "disks."

PRACTICE WORDS AND SENTENCES.   Use the same procedure for the following:

asks	risks	masks
frisks	basks	tusks
desks	tasks	flasks

Weigh all the risks.

When will the tasks be completed?

She never asks for much.

The disks are on the desks.

GETTING THE RIGHT "T" SOUND

Very often words like "written" and "button" get swallowed and sound more like "wri—en" and "buh—on." Many speakers are unsure of just how much "t" sound to give words such as these. If the "t" in "written" is given a strong articulation (as in "*t*en"), the word will come out sounding unnatural and contrived. On the other hand, many speakers never articulate the "t" sound at all. Instead, they abruptly stop after the first vowel (wri:) and then add the "en" ending as in "wri//en." Stopping short between the two vowel sounds is what creates the swallowing effect.

PRACTICE EXERCISE: WRITTEN.   Say "writ." When you get to the "t" sound, leave the tip of your tongue on the roof of your mouth. Repeat the sound "writ." Keeping your tongue on the roof of the mouth, simply add the "n" sound and say "writ'n." The tongue tip should stay up on the roof of your mouth until the entire word has ended. Repeat the word "written."

PRACTICE WORDS AND SENTENCES

button	cotton	mitten	typewritten
flatten	eaten	sweeten	curtain
rotten	fatten	tighten	carton
satin	heighten	certainly	Martin
bitten	kitten	forgotten	important
Britain	Latin	unbeaten	

On the word "important," make sure to release the tongue tip on the final "t."

He's written about the Latin culture.

This must be sweetened before it can be eaten.

Sew the button on the satin blouse.

Does Britain import much cotton?

The kitten was certainly not forgotten.

It was heightened without the curtain.

HOW TO PRONOUNCE "R" SOUNDS CORRECTLY

Are you an "r-dropper" or an "r-adder?" Well, if "morning" sounds more like "mawning" or "idea" sounds more like "idear," then you've just tested positive to one or both groups.

Dropping or adding an "r" where it doesn't belong is a very common problem with this consonant. These kinds of mistakes can be heard in New York City and many sections of New England, as well as parts of the South. Many Asian speakers also have difficulties with "r" sounds.

Don't Drop Your "R"

If you're a native speaker of English, you probably won't have trouble pronouncing "r" when it begins a word, as in "run." But the "r" tends to get dropped when it follows a vowel. This can happen in the middle of a word, as in "st*aht*" instead of "sta*r*t," or at the end of a word, as in "fl*aw*" instead of "floo*r*."

The Final "R" Sound

If you can pronounce the initial "r" in "*r*un," you should also be able to say the "r" in "barrel" or in "star." After all, the "r" sound is basically made the same way whether it comes at the beginning, middle, or end of a word.

PRACTICE EXERCISE: RUNNER.   Begin by saying "run," paying attention to the way the muscles of your mouth and throat feel as you pronounce the first sound. Then add the final "r." Let the tongue pull back slightly inside the mouth and feel the sound vibrate in the back of the mouth and throat as you say that final "r." For non-native speakers of English, think of growling out the "r" sound. Once the sound is established, the growling effect can be softened or eliminated.

PRACTICE WORDS AND SENTENCES

car	pure	far	air
jar	care	dear	prepare
hear	impair	career	messenger
near	letter	door	under
more	answer	ignore	retainer
explore	recover	sure	are
cure	bar	insure	seminar

PRACTICE WORDS AND SENTENCES, cont'd.

beer	clear	consider	fare
sincere	score	star	repair
four	floor	fear	rare
soar	secure	appear	matter
tour	lure	before	producer
you're	there	core	pressure
tar	airfare	endure	September
cigar	elevator	poor	tender
year	lecture	where	offer

Are you getting to the seminar by car?

It's clear he's near the end of his career.

We need four more doors.

You're secure on this tour.

This software can't compare.

We were about to refer her.

Send the letter by messenger.

What's the matter with the elevator?

The producer has no answer.

I'm under a lot of pressure.

The lecture is never in September.

We must recover the retainer.

Let's consider the tender offer.

The Medial "R" Sound

Like "r" sounds at the beginnings or ends of words, an "r" *inside* words can also cause problems. Usually this is because they occur just before another consonant.

PRACTICE EXERCISE: FARM.   Begin by saying the word "far." Don't let the "r" die away; keep it going. Now close your lips and add the final "m." Repeat "farrrrr-m," paying attention to the way the muscles in your mouth feel during the "r-m" sequence. Now say it again, quickly: "farm."

PRACTICE WORDS AND SENTENCES

alarm	order	worst	dealership
Harvard	board	merge	scholarship
party	ordinary	appeared	intercom
concern	endorsed	carefully	interface
serve	farm	fortune	reservation
earn	large	court	membership
beard	chart	mortgage	energy
airline	certainly	absorb	Saturday
quarter	person	partner	overtime
warning	convert	part	yesterday
important	clearly	Arkansas	interval
incorporate	farewell	work	alternate
Carmen	support	turn	supervise
hard	afford	third	property
start	forty	nearby	neighborhood
learn	performance	New York	afterthought
word	harmony	overcome	otherwise
immerse	market	enterprise	conversation
weird	target	letterhead	observation
chairman	first	advertise	international

Always target a large market.

She's always the first person to work.

It appeared that the check had cleared.

PRACTICE WORDS AND SENTENCES, cont'd.

They took forty orders in New York.

The chairman went to the airport.

Yesterday was Saturday.

You can't advertise this property.

We must underwrite the scholarship.

The conversation was hard to understand.

The supervisor was working overtime.

Use an alternate energy source.

Don't Add an "R" Where It Doesn't Belong

Oddly enough, many "r-droppers" are also "r-adders." This intrusive "r" (an "r" sound where it doesn't belong) mostly affects speakers from sections of New York and New England. The problem occurs most often in words ending with an "aw" sound (when "s*aw*" becomes "sore"), and words that end with an "uh" sound (when "sod*a*" becomes "soder"). To eliminate this, keep the mouth and tongue completely still on the final vowel sound. If the lips and tongue close too soon, the "r" sound will enter in.

PRACTICE EXERCISE: LAW.   Say the word "law."

1. When you hit the final "aw" sound, FREEZE.
2. Don't move your lips, tongue, or jaw.
3. Repeat the word "law."

Keeping the lips and tongue perfectly still on the final vowel will automatically prevent the "r" sound from sneaking in.

PRACTICE WORDS AND SENTENCES ENDING IN "AW."   (In the following exercise, notice the difference between words ending in "r" and words ending in "aw.")

sore	saw
drawer	draw
roar	raw
pour	paw
floor	flaw
nor	gnaw
oar	awe
lore	law
shore	Shaw
straw	thaw
jaw	withdraw
Arkansas	Nassau

My son-in-law is from Arkansas.

We saw only one flaw.

Mr. Shaw had to withdraw.

PRACTICE WORDS AND SENTENCES ENDING IN "UH." In the following exercise, differentiate between words ending in "r" and words ending in "uh."

error	era
calmer	comma
diner	Dinah
leaner	Lena
tamper	Tampa
wander	Wanda
moaner	Mona
Peter	pita

Pᴀᴄᴛɪᴄᴇ Wᴏʀᴅs ᴀɴᴅ Sᴇɴᴛᴇɴᴄᴇs Eɴᴅɪɴɢ ɪɴ "UH," cont'd

soda	criteria	area
idea	agenda	umbrella
America	vanilla	quota
diploma	data	gala
formula	visa	Carolina
stamina	Virginia	Jamaica
sofa	dilemma	media

America is big on multimedia.

Don't spill soda on the sofa.

There's no data in this area.

I have an idea for the agenda.

Also avoid the extra "r" sound in words such as:

Correct	*Incorrect*
offer	orfer
wash	warsh
Washington	Warshington

GETTING THROUGH THICK AND THIN

Does "*th*ree of *th*ose" sound more like "*t*ree of *d*oze?" While substituting "t" or "d" for the "th" sound is generally considered part of the New York City dialect, occasionally this can be heard in other major urban areas of the country as well. At times, the "diss," "deeze," "dat's," and "doze" can all take on a rather crude and unsophisticated sound; the kind of sound that's associated with a "tough-guy" manner of speaking or street talk. This often creates an uneducated impression and certainly won't help your career.

Also, since the "th" sound is absent from many other languages, many foreigners have a great deal of difficulty incorporating this sound into their everyday speech. Many non-native speakers of English also substitute "s" or "z" for the "th" sound, so depending on your accent, "*th*at is wor*th*" may sound more like "*z*at is wor*s*e." Some speakers may also substitute "f" or "v" for the "th" sound so "bo*th* of *th*ese" may sound like "boh*f* of *v*eez."

Making the "TH" Sound

Place the tip of your tongue between your teeth. This means you must actually stick your tongue out ever so slightly when making the "th" sound. If the tip of your tongue stays inside the mouth you're not making the correct sound. There are actually two types of "th" sounds, the voiced "th" and the voiceless "th." The voiced "th" is made with the vocal cords vibrating; the voiceless "th" is made without that vibration. The tongue position is the same for both "th" sounds.

Because these two sounds (like "s" and "z") can be kept going a while, you can easily check to see which one you are actually making. Put your fingertips against the front of your throat, say the "th" in "there" or "mother," and keep the sound going. When you're making the right sound, you will feel your vocal cords vibrating under your fingers. Now do the same thing with the "th" sound in "think" or "bath"; when you make the right sound, you will feel no vibration. (If you have trouble doing this, try it with "zzzzzzzzzzzzzzzz," which is voiced and produces a vibration that you can feel with your fingers, and then with "ssssssssssssssss," which is voiceless and produces no vibration. Then follow exactly the same process with the two "th" sounds.)

Voiced "TH" Practice Exercise: Then

1. Place the tip of the tongue between your teeth.
2. Sound the voice and feel the vibration on the tongue tip and teeth as you make the "th" sound.
3. Be sure you're not saying "den" or "zen."
4. Repeat the word "then."

Voiceless "TH" Practice Exercise: Thank

1. Place the tongue tip between your teeth.
2. Gently push out the breath on the "th" sound and say "thank."
3. Make sure you're not saying "tank" or "sank."
4. Repeat the word "thank."

Using the Voiced "TH" Correctly

Differentiate between the following groups of words:

Dan/van	than
den	then
dare	there
day	they
Dale/veil	they'll
Dave	they've
doze	those
dough	though
ladder	lather
breed/breeze	breathe

PRACTICE WORDS AND PHRASES

At the Beginning of the Word

the	thus	therefore
that	these	this
themselves	them	thereby

They have these over there.

We told them to do this.

That was easier than the rest.

Inside the Word

other	trustworthy
either	another
mother	brother
neither	gather
wither	smoother
further	otherwise
togetherness	worthy
weather	altogether
bother	together
clothing	father
rather	leather
nevertheless	southern
furthermore	

Neither of them was together.

I'd rather have another.

Don't bother going any further.

My father loves the weather.

The southern brother gathered the leather clothing.

At the End of the Word

bathe	breathe	clothe	loathe
smooth	soothe		

Please bathe and clothe the child.

I loathe a smooth character.

Breathe deeply to soothe yourself.

Using the Voiceless "TH" Sound Correctly

Place the tip of the tongue between the teeth and gently push out the breath on the voiceless "th" sound. Differentiate between the following groups of words:

tank/sank	thank
team/seam	theme
tick/sick	thick
tie/sigh	thigh
tin/sin/fin	thin
ting/sing	thing
taught/sought/fought	thought
tread	thread
tree/free	three
true	through
trust	thrust
tug	thug
saw	thaw
sink/fink	think
sum	thumb
pat/pass	path
bat/bass	bath
boot	booth
boat	both
brought	broth
debt/deaf	death
fate/face	faith
wit	with
mat/mass	math
toot	tooth
root/roof	Ruth

oat/oaf	oath
fort/force	forth
Bert	birth
mit/miss/miff	myth
mouse	mouth
worse	worth

PRACTICE WORDS AND SENTENCES

At the Beginning of the Word

thirty	three-thirty	third	thirty-third
thesis	thaw	theft	thorough
Thursday	thousand	theater	threat
thruway	throughout	threshold	

We thought her thesis was thorough.

I think it's Thursday at three-thirty.

The thrift shop was thriving along the Thruway.

Thank you for going through the theater.

Inside the Word

author	ethics	lethal	mouthful
bathroom	ruthless	northeast	toothbrush
withdraw	withhold	withstand	worthless
worthwhile	nothing	something	authorize
faithfully	sympathy	synthetic	enthusiastic
cutthroat	enthrall	overthrow	
afterthought	forthcoming	birthday	

Kathy authorized the withdrawal.

The author wrote nothing about ethics.

We're enthusiastic about the forthcoming meeting.

Something is wrong with the bathroom.

At the End of the Word

width	underneath	truth	breath
growth	length	mouth	health
south	warmth	month	depth
strength	fifth	sixth	eighteenth
north	one-hundredth	Meredith	Kenneth
Edith	earth	youth	

Tell us the truth about your health.

What is the growth fund really worth?

He traveled the earth, north and south.

Both of us led the youth down the path.

Ruth was in her ninth month of pregnancy.

DON'T DROP YOUR G'S—THE "ING" ENDINGS

If you are from the South, the Midwest, or New York City, or if Spanish is your native language, there's a good chance that you may be substituting "in" for "ing" in words like "calling" or "going." The "ng" sound in "ing" is actually only one consonant sound, just like "b" or "m." But because we write "ng" with two letters, it's customary to say that people who use "callin" and "goin" for "calling" and "going" are *dropping* the "g" endings. We will follow that practice here, for simplicity's sake.

The problem of dropping the "g" has nothing at all to do with the difficulty of *pronouncing* the "ing" sequence. If that was the problem, people who had it would say "rin" for "ring" and "brin" for "bring"; that never happens. It's just a matter of remembering that for Standard

English the "ing" of "falling" is just as important as the "ing" sequence in "ring" or "bring" and must be pronounced in exactly the same way.

Practice Sentences

There's no telling what they're planning.

She's speaking at the beginning of the meeting.

We were thinking of starting in the morning.

You're going to be fighting a losing battle.

He's hoping to do something in banking.

We're counting on you to do the talking.

I'm calling regarding the managing position.

Pronounce It Correctly!
Beware of Common Mispronunciations

In addition to all the problem pronunciations discussed above, there are quite a few individual English words that are frequently mispronounced. You will want to learn to give them the Standard English pronunciation. The list that follows contains the most troublesome examples; the more Standard English versions you can add to your speech, the better you will sound.

Nonstandard	*Standard*
govner	gove*r*nor
goverment	gove*r*nment
probly	prob*ab*ly
are	our (hour)
axe	a*sk*
excape	escape

Nonstandard	*Standard*
expecially	especially
samwich	sandwich
liberry	library
fur	for
with	width
mist	midst
pitcher	picture (pick-cher)
Febrary or Feberry	February (Feb-roo-er-ee)
pronounciation	pronunciation
interpert	interpret
tempature	temperature (tem-pra-chur)
real-a-tor	realtor (real-tor)
spose	suppose
sposely	supposedly
reconize	recognize
expertees	expertise (ek-spur-teez)
sosal	social (soh-shul)
boh-teek	boutique (boo-teek)
ne-goh-see-ayt	negotiate (ne-goh-shee-ayt)
cuz	because (be-kawz)
speh-shee-a-li-tee	specialty (speh-shul-tee)
disorientated	disoriented
off-ten	often (off-en)
baysilly	basically (bay-sick-ly)
espress	express
artic	arctic (ark-tic)
bin-ess	business (biz-ness)
mis-chée-vee-us	mischievous (mís-chuh-vus)
akerit	accurate (a-cure-it)

Nonstandard	Standard
susess	success (suck-sess)
asept	accept (ak-sept)
ekcetra	et cetera (et-set-er-a)
vice-a-versa	vice versa
strenth	stre*ng*th
lenth	le*ng*th
nu-kya-ler	nuclear (nu-klee-er)
reglar	reg*u*lar
hung*r*y	Hung*a*ry
nut'n	nothing
suh'm	something
pre-fér-a-ble	preferable (pré-fer-a-ble)
a-plíck-a-ble	applicable (á-plick-a-ble)
com-páir-a-ble	comparable (cóm-per-a-ble)
ir-re-páir-a-ble	irreparable (ir-rép-er-a-ble)
for-míd-a-ble	formidable (fór-mid-a-ble)
chazim	chasm (ka-zim)

How to Avoid Other Obstacles to Clear Speaking

As strange as it may seem, many people whose pronunciation is completely standard, forget some of the most basic rules of clear speaking. Here are a few:

1. Avoid talking with your hand in front of your mouth; it interferes with the quality of your speech and muffles your sound.

2. You shouldn't have anything in your mouth—a pipe, toothpick, gum, candy, or food when speaking. If you're having lunch and the phone rings, make sure to answer it with an empty mouth. Let's face it, nobody wants to hear you talk with your mouth full.

3. Get rid of junk words. *"Like, ya know,* fillers are really annoying *and stuff, okay?"* It's been called "Valley Girl Speak" or "Teen Speak" when junk words such as these dominate a person's speech. While an occasional "ya know" or "uhm" is not the end of the world, using fillers excessively weakens your message and can distract your listener. To prove this point, say the following sentence aloud: *"Like* we either change our strategy, *ya know,* or lose the business, *okay?"* Now take away the fillers and say the same sentence: "We either change our strategy, or lose the business." Which message is clearer? Which statement makes a stronger impact?

How often do junk words pop up in your speech? The answer may surprise you. In the course of a half-hour lesson, a student of mine once used "likes" and "ya knows" 103 times! Here's a simple test you can run to find out just how high your "filler count" is. Record yourself during a series of telephone conversations at home or at work. At the end of a day, play back the tape and start counting. If you have a bad case of "likes" and "ya knows" here are a few techniques to help remove them:

- *Replace fillers with brief pauses.* Many people fear silence and use junk words to fill up empty space. Remember, pausing from time to time gives you a chance to think your ideas through and helps listeners absorb information.

- *Slow down.* Rapid speakers are generally more prone to using fillers. The faster you speak, the less time you have to think about what you're saying. The less time you have to edit your speech, the easier it is for junk words to enter in. Slowing down gives you more time to concentrate on each thought. This way, you won't need to rely on fillers.

- *Use visual aids.* Post a sticker by your telephone displaying your most common fillers. This way, each time you talk on the phone you'll have a visual reminder of what not to say. Even when you're away from the phone, there are visual aids you can use. Try wearing something a little out of the ordinary. For example, if you normally wear a watch, ring, or bracelet on your left hand, try switching it to the right hand. This will be obvious to you but not to others. You'll find that changing a dress habit can help trigger the awareness of your speech habit.

Remember, whenever you feel the urge to say "like" or "ya know," give yourself a moment of silence instead. As your awareness increases, these silent gaps should begin to disappear, allowing your thoughts to flow freely and uninterrupted.

Say It Out Loud!

Here are six brief quotations that you can read aloud (and/or memorize to say aloud without reading) as a way to practice what you've learned in this chapter. Concentrate on clear and distinct pronunciation as you go through each excerpt.

> *If your back is up against the wall, it is not quite as difficult to come up with the right answers. You do the job or you're dead.*
>
> W.R. TIMKEN,
> quoted in Reed Abelson et al., "Corporate Leaders: Is There a Doctor in the House?," *Forbes* Magazine, May 28, 1990, p. 226.

> *Entrepreneurial businesses stumble onto something, get a big boost out of it, and grow significantly. Then, as soon as they think they're rounding third base, someone always seems to move home plate.*
>
> DAVID L. BIRCH,
> "What Goes Up . . . ," *Inc.* Magazine, July 1988, p. 25.

> *As a hypothetical illustration, consider Lincoln's* Gettysburg Address *as it might have been written by Dwight Eisenhower, probably beginning something like "Eighty-seven years ago, I think it was."*
>
> RONALD H. CARPENTER,
> "The Problem of Style in Presidential Discourse," in *Concepts in Communication,* edited by Jimmie D. Trent, Judith S. Trent, and Daniel J. O'Neill; Allyn and Bacon, Inc., 1973, p. 110.

Imagine if Tom Brokaw or Peter Jennings came on the air to announce that there was really no significant news today, and that there would be a 20-minute interlude of Beethoven sonatas instead. Honest? Yes. Economically suicidal? Also yes.

THOMAS SOWELL,
"Observations: Just Words," *Forbes* Magazine, February 13, 1995, p. 109.

At the risk of oversimplifying, big and small shareholders may now communicate freely with each other without fear of breaking proxy solicitation rules, disclosure rules and who knows what other rules, thereby creating a litigation and regulatory quagmire.

FREDERICK E. ROWE, JR.,
"Hurrah for October 15," *Forbes* Magazine, February 15, 1993, p. 234.

I never make small propositions. It's just as difficult to move the water cooler from one end of the corridor to the other as it is to change the basic nature of a business.

PETER DRUCKER,
quoted in Elizabeth Hall, "A Conversation With Peter F. Drucker," *Psychology Today*, December 1982, p. 64.

3

Getting Rid of Speech That's Too Fast or Too Slow to Make Yourself Understood

HOW RAPID-FIRE SPEECH CAN SPOIL THE PICTURE

Chelsea Henderson looked around the gallery with real satisfaction; everything looked great. The hours spent getting ready for this show had obviously been well spent. Both of her assistants had been busy all morning moving from one cluster of potential buyers to another. The cheerful hum she heard coming from all directions told her that Aron and Lisa were doing well, building the kind of enthusiastic good mood that made people pull out their checkbooks and credit cards to buy things.

But the crowd was getting too big for them! Chelsea could see that one couple was getting restless; they kept looking around for someone to talk to about the big seascape by the front window, a piece she'd been trying to sell for almost a year. *I'm not about to let them get away!* she thought, and she set down the catalogs she'd been sorting and headed for the couple, wearing her most elegant welcoming smile.

To her dismay—but not surprise—Lisa headed her off after abruptly abandoning her own sales prospects. "Chelsea," she said, "have you finished sorting those catalogs?"

Chelsea frowned. "No," she said, "but there's no hurry—"

"You're wrong!" the other woman told her firmly, taking her elbow and moving her skillfully back toward the long display table. "It really can't wait—remember, I told you that when we came in this morning."

"But, Lisa, that couple over there—"

"I'll get to them right away, Chelsea. I promise."

It was no use struggling—unless Chelsea wanted to make a scene right in the middle of her show. Lisa maneuvered her boss toward the stack of catalogs, asked her to please stay there and finish the task, and disappeared.

It's happening again, Chelsea thought miserably. She was once again going to have to fire another otherwise excellent assistant. What was the matter with them, anyway? They were all bright and willing and skilled, but she couldn't seem to find anybody who didn't start trying to take over the gallery after the first week! Aron and Lisa were no exception; neither of them would let her go near a customer. As if this were *their* gallery instead of hers! The thought of more firing and hiring made her head ache, but what else could she do?

What else could she do? Well, for one thing, she could use her common sense. It's just not likely that every single assistant she hires will fight to keep her away from customers because of a lust for power. There has to be another explanation. But because Chelsea knows she is always superbly dressed and groomed and fresh—not one of those awful people with their hair falling down and bad breath and their clothes all wrinkled—it never crosses her mind that she could be the source of the problem. She would be stunned to learn that if she sat her assistants down and refused to let them go until they explained their behavior, this is what they would say:

"Chelsea, you're a good businesswoman and you really know art. But people can't stand the way you *talk!* You talk so fast that they can't understand you, and you make feel like they're under fire or something! Haven't you noticed? When people see you heading their way, they just *leave.* If we let you talk to them, we wouldn't have any customers!"

That message would hurt Chelsea deeply, but it's too bad that she hasn't had a chance to hear it. As long as she remains unaware of her problem, she will continue to face other difficulties that are equally hurtful. And the problem would be just as bad if she spoke much more slowly than the average person, instead of more rapidly.

TOO FAST? TOO SLOW? TOO BAD!

Speech that is either too fast or too slow is difficult to understand and frustrating to listen to; it's sure to spoil business deals and lose sales. If you talk too fast, people have to struggle to understand your words and they feel as if you're trying to con them out of something; they perceive you as somebody who can't be trusted. If you talk too slow, they still have to struggle, because waiting for your next word to come along annoys them and interferes with their ability to understand what you're saying. Your *working memory*—the part of your brain that processes incoming information for action, discard, or storage—is badly handicapped by a stream of speech that deviates drastically from the norm for your native language. And people are likely to assume that very slow speech goes with very slow thinking; they may perceive you as not very bright. Being perceived as either untrustworthy or unintelligent is certainly not going to help you get ahead!

How to Determine Whether You Speak Too Rapidly or Too Slowly

Obviously you don't want to make an effort to speak more slowly (or more quickly) if you don't need to. Your first step, then, is to find out how your speech rate compares with that of other people. It's hard to judge this for yourself, because your own rate of speech *feels* right to you. There are three things you can do as a way of checking this:

1. Go to a friend or associate whose speech you admire and whose judgment you respect, and ask: "What's your opinion about my speed when I talk? Do you think I talk too fast, or too slow—or is it okay?"

2. Ask that same friend or associate to tape one of the short sample speeches in the appendix to this book; then tape that same speech yourself. (Or make a tape on which you record the same brief speech that appears on a tape by some respected public speaker.) Time the two tapes and compare them. If there is a large difference—if your tape is a lot longer or shorter than the other one—that will give you some evidence about your own speech rate.

3. Listen very carefully to a tape of yourself in conversation with a friend or family member. When you have another person's rate of speech to compare with your own, it may help you decide whether you speak too quickly or too slowly.

None of these steps is foolproof, because it may be that the *other* person is the one whose speech rate needs changing! Or all the people involved may speak a dialect with a speech rate that differs from the average. Many New Yorkers, for example, talk very fast, while people from the deep South often speak extremely slowly. Common sense will help you here. If your own speech is annoying or frustrating to other people, you're probably already aware of that, although you may not have understood why. Similarly, if the person whose speech you're comparing with your own is someone everybody seems to enjoy listening to (or is a professional speaker they'll pay money to listen to) that person almost certainly has an acceptable speech rate.

Bringing Rapid-Fire Speech Under Control

Some speech teachers say that a person's optimal rate of speech is about 150 words per minute. That's like saying that the best driving speed is about 55 miles per hour. Obviously, different levels of ability as well as changing driving conditions would make it impossible to adhere to any one speed. Our speech pattern works in much the same way. There's no such thing as a "national speech limit." Good speakers come in all speeds. What works for one person may not necessarily work for another. Henry Kissinger speaks effectively using a slow rate of speech (because of a medical problem) while Ross Perot does well with a quicker pace. Your goal is to find a speed that allows for clear and distinct pronunciation. The main point is that people have to be able to understand you. Since certain speakers can enunciate clearly at higher speeds than others, this will differ from person to person. It also differs from one English dialect to another.

WHY DO PEOPLE RUSH THEIR SPEECH?

In general, most people tend to speak too quickly. There are several reasons for this. Take a look and see if you fall into any of the categories listed.

Speaking Slowly Might Cause Loss of Interest

People often think, "If I don't go fast enough, listeners will lose interest." This is rarely the case. In fact, the chance of losing your audience is greater if you speak too quickly because they may not be able to keep up with you. Many speakers rattle along not realizing that their thoughts and ideas are being heard for the very first time. As a result, listeners often don't get enough time to absorb the new material and their attention may wander.

Nervousness Can Cause Rapid Speech

As your body gets charged up with adrenaline, your speech usually accelerates as well. A software executive was once astonished when she heard a recording of her presentation during a national sales convention. Despite some jitters at the podium, her pacing felt perfectly normal to her; but on the recording her words flew by like a runaway locomotive. To control your pace, say the following three words to yourself: "LET THEM WAIT." Making your audience wait for you puts you in the driver's seat and helps give you a better sense of control. And there's an added benefit: when you sound relaxed, your audience relaxes with you.

Our Speech Reflects Our Fast-Paced World

As our society becomes more high-tech, it seems to become more hectic as well. Automation was supposed to give us more leisure time but instead it's made us work longer, harder, and faster. Now, more is expected of us in less time. With the advent of personal computers, laser printers, and fax machines, as well as the barrage of images we see on video, information is being delivered in a flash. It's easy to get caught up in this whirlwind of activity, and our rate of speech is no exception. Keep in mind that the human speech mechanism is not a high-tech instrument. It requires a relatively slow operating speed to communicate clearly and effectively.

Psychological Factors Can Speed Up Speech

We've all heard people whose minds go faster than their speech. They cram too much into each breath and must rush their speech to complete the thought. Concentrating on one thought at a time and using fewer words in each breath can help overcome this problem.

GETTING RID OF POOR PHRASING
TO CORRECT YOUR RATE OF SPEECH

Another factor that can cause you to speak too quickly or too slowly is the speech problem called *poor phrasing*. Taking a breath at the wrong place, or failing to breathe often enough, or taking too many breaths—any of these can give you a speech rate that makes a bad impression on others. Let's discuss this problem in some detail; it's important, and it may be something you've never given much thought to before.

A phrase is a word or group of words spoken as a unit and separated from the stream of speech by pauses. A single phrase is spoken in one breath. Learning how to phrase well can significantly affect your pace as well as your message.

Before you can speak in phrases you must first be able to think in phrases. This means you must determine how much you can comfortably say in each breath without losing the continuity or logic of your thought. Many speakers don't pay much attention to phrasing. They simply take a breath whenever they run out of air. This can lead to all kinds of problems, from gasping to a weak and breathy sound.

A CEO in the health-care industry complained that whenever he gave a speech his voice would die out prematurely. The ends of his sentences would trail off, causing his voice to lose its energy and enthusiasm. It sounded as though the life was being sucked out of his delivery. By learning to speak in shorter phrases and pausing for breaths as he spoke, he was able to sustain his sentences with more power and regain the vocal vitality he had lost.

How you group words together can also affect the clarity of your message. Letting your thoughts ramble on without clearly separating your ideas can easily cloud the meaning of your message. It's kind of like a run-on sentence. Stringing together too many ideas in one sentence can make your writing unclear, and confuse your readers. While we're taught to avoid run-on sentences when we write, little, if anything, is said about how to prevent run-on thoughts when we speak.

Remember, the key to good phrasing is learning how to *think* in phrases. As a rule, most people don't pause enough when they speak. As they form an idea in their head, they feel compelled to communicate the entire thought to their listener all at once without stopping. Their speech gets faster and faster, and before you know it, they're already on to the next thought, although the listener is still trying to absorb the initial idea. So, to control your pace and articulate your thoughts clearly, you'll find that a single thought or idea may need to be subdivided into two, three, or four parts, depending on the length and complexity of the thought.

USING PAUSES TO MAKE YOUR SPEECH EASIER TO UNDERSTAND

Just as commas are used to separate ideas within a sentence, pauses help to break down your thoughts into more manageable units when you speak. This makes your message easier to listen to, and much easier to understand. Simply put, think of adding commas as you speak. Here are a few guidelines to help you determine when and where to add pauses in your speech.

1. Use pauses after phrases that begin with prepositions and adverbs. For example:

   • By the time you get to New York, (pause) the meeting will be underway.

   • Despite all our efforts, (pause) we were unable to get the account.

   • Even if we had the resources, (pause) it wouldn't make sense to go ahead with this project.

2. Use pauses when running down a list of items. To help your listener better absorb information, it's a good idea to add a short pause after each item in a series. For example:

   • We need to relocate our offices, (pause) open two new branches, (pause) interview qualified job applicants, (pause) and hire 20 additional employees.

   • I want to review the research and development process, (pause) the new marketing strategy, (pause) as well as the distribution system.

3. Use pauses before connecting words such as "but," "or," "and," "because," "however," and so on. For example:

   • Diane is basically a good employee; (pause) however, she does have a lateness problem.

   • I told them to put their money in bonds, (pause) because they wanted a low-risk investment.

Keep in mind that when speaking from a written text, you can't always follow the printed punctuation. Many speakers pause for a breath whenever they see a comma, colon, or semicolon. But a long written sequence may contain too many words to speak comfortably in one breath. When this happens, you'll need to break it down into smaller sections and write in some extra punctuation marks to indicate where to pause for a breath. As a rule, the longer the statement, the more pauses you'll have to make.

The following statement is divided into four separate word groups or phrases. Say the statement out loud and notice how the pauses help enhance the message.

"We met with the committee yesterday, (pause) and we all agreed (pause) that for our company to remain competitive, (pause) we need to develop a new business strategy."

Many nonstop talkers are afraid of pausing for breaths as they speak because they fear the moments of silence might make them lose their train of thought. First of all, the kind of pauses we're talking about only last a split second. More importantly, pausing for breaths as you speak improves your phrasing, and good phrasing actually helps you to organize your thoughts and ideas. You'll think more clearly and sound clearer, too.

Learning to punctuate your speech can also help when you have to talk extemporaneously. If you have a habit of cramming too many words into each breath, think of adding commas as you go along. Then pause for a breath after each comma. This will help slow you down just as periodically tapping the brakes of a car regulates the speed.

ADJUSTING YOUR PACE TO MEET ANY CHALLENGE

Good speakers use a flexible rate of speech. They adjust their pace and phrasing to meet the needs of any given situation. Here are some examples:

The Size of the Speaking Environment

As a rule, it's a good idea to talk slowly and use short phrases when you have to speak in a large space. This is really a matter of acoustics. Sound needs more time to travel through a large auditorium than through a small room. Slowing down is particularly important when speaking outdoors, where a lot of your sound can get lost.

Speaking with Amplification

If you've ever heard a message come over an echoey public address system (New York City subway stations would provide a good example), then you know what a jumbled mess it can sound like. When your voice is amplified over a powerful audio system, be prepared for the sound to reverberate. The more amplification, the more reverberations you can expect. This echoing effect can cause your words to overlap each other and garble your message. To prevent this from happening, use short phrases and allow ample time for pauses as you speak. When addressing a large group without a microphone, speaking in short phrases can help to project the voice. Putting fewer words in each breath gives you more time to fill out and sustain your phrases.

Leaving Recorded Telephone Messages

Many people tend to speak too fast on the phone. This is especially true when leaving your name or company name and phone number. When giving a phone number, people often rush through the entire number plus area code all in one breath. No wonder so many wrong numbers are dialed! The best way to give a phone number is to phrase it in four distinct units. Pause after the area code, and pause again after the first three numbers, then say the final four numbers in groups of two. For example, if the phone number is (212) 123-4567, then phrase it as follows: 212(pause)-123(pause)-45(pause)67. This will make it crystal clear to your listener.

Remember, a machine can't ask you to repeat yourself if you don't speak clearly the first time around. And a sloppy message could make the difference between getting your call returned or not.

Making Cold Sales Calls

Salespeople are often taught to match the speaking tempo of their prospects, especially when talking on the telephone. The theory is that being sensitive to your customer's pace helps create good rapport and can make you sound "in sync" with the person you are talking to. When communicating with a slow speaker, you may need to slow down a bit to adjust to his or her speed. However, when you come up against a fast talker, be careful not to go beyond your personal speed limit! For example, if you're making a sales pitch to someone who sounds in a rush, it's better to shorten your pitch and speak clearly than to race through the entire presentation and risk sounding out of control. (This is also a good way of getting a fast talker to adjust to *your* pace.)

Emphasizing Key Points

To speak convincingly, you also need to adjust your pace according to the significance of the thought you're trying to convey. The more important the thought, the more time you should take to express it. Imagine you were on a sightseeing tour. Wouldn't you want to slow down to observe the key attractions? However, many speakers use the same rate of speech regardless of what they are trying to communicate. As a result, they often "throw away" the most important words of their message and weaken its impact. Remember, not all words are created equal. Slowing down on key words and phrases creates emphasis and can really help to drive home a significant point.

Keep in mind that the rate of your speech can determine the way others respond to your ideas. If you speak too quickly, people may think that what you're saying isn't that important. After all, if *you* don't think it's worth taking the time to express yourself clearly, why should others take the time to listen? So take the time you need to make it count; don't be afraid to slow yourself down. Many people frown at the thought of having to slow down because they think a slower speed lacks energy and enthusiasm. On the contrary, using a moderate pace allows you to articulate your thoughts clearly, and clarity has vitality. Slow and clean sounds a lot better than fast and sloppy! Also, speaking at a moderate tempo allows sound to resonate better and can actually enrich the quality of your voice. In short, taking your time can make you sound much more confident.

As stated at the beginning of this chapter, the overwhelming tendency of most people is to speak too quickly. There are far fewer people who speak too slowly. Because many believe that slow talkers sound boring, speeding up is often prescribed as a quick-fix cure. Usually it's not an effective treatment, however. In most cases, it's not the *speed* that makes slow speakers sound boring; it's more often a *lack of variety* that's the problem. Remember: motion alone doesn't add emotion. With the right rate of speech, neither too fast nor too slow, as well as a variety of pacing, you can hold the interest of your listeners.

Say It Out Loud!

Here are five brief quotations that you can read aloud (and/or memorize to say aloud without reading) as a way to practice what you've learned in this chapter. Punctuate your speech with pauses as you try out each excerpt.

> *Among all the professions, only two or three others can compare with political leadership in its demands that the individual be able to think one thing and yet, within certain ethical and practical boundaries, say something quite different.*
>
> Hedley Donovan,
> "The Enigmatic President," *Time* Magazine, May 6, 1985, p. 29.

> *It is often said that the difference between American and Japanese business attitudes is that Americans plan for the next quarter while the Japanese plan for eternity.*
>
> Michael M. Lewis,
> "The Money Culture: Japanese Takeout," *The New Republic,*
> October 3, 1988, p. 19.

> *If the poor believe that most wealthy people are exploiters and thieves who squash other people into poverty for personal gain, they will not be likely to climb the ladder of economic success.*
>
> Michael Bauman,
> "The Dangerous Samaritans: How We Unintentionally Injure the Poor,"
> *Imprimis,* January 1994, p. 2.

In the past many chief executives liked to pack their board rooms with trusted allies . . . But those days are numbered. The trend is for more directors with specialized skills and experience who have fewer ties to management.

Brigid McMenamin,
"Help Wanted," *Forbes* Magazine, November 22, 1993, p. 186.

In Search of Excellence . . . *can be summed up in one sentence: Being a good human being is good business.*

Paul Hawken,
"Surviving in Small Businesses," *Coevolution Quarterly,*
Spring 1984, p. 17.

4

Getting Rid of Unwanted Voices That Could Hold You Back

HOW A WHINING, NASAL VOICE CAN BREAK A LEASE

Marilyn Lee had been waiting several days to talk with Gary Hendron about the upcoming move, and she was relieved to see that he had shown *up* this time. Twice before, he'd made an appointment for their meeting and then broken it, which wasn't like him at all. Gary was usually the most considerate and courteous of men. During the six years that he had leased space from her law firm, there had never once been a disagreement of any kind. Now that he was in her office at last, she got straight to the point.

"Gary," she said, "I'm glad you could finally make it, because we need your decision. I have the floor plans for our new location right here." She laid them on the desk in front of him. "The space we can offer you is the one marked with the red X—you remember I told you about it last week. It's not fancy, but it's convenient, it has plenty of room, and it has three nice windows. Can I assume that you'll be moving with us?"

Gary cleared his throat, but he said nothing, and he didn't look down at the plans.

"Is there a problem?" Marilyn asked him when she realized that the silence was going to go on and on unless she broke it herself. "Is something wrong?"

"Marilyn," he said slowly, avoiding her eyes, "I do remember talking about this. I also remember you telling me that that space is the *only* one you can give me, and that none of the other room assignments is negotiable, either."

"That's right," she answered. "I'm sorry about that, but it's the only possible arrangement. I don't understand, though . . . It's a larger area than the one you're leasing from us now, and a lot nicer. I thought you *wanted* to be closer to downtown."

"Marilyn," he said, "I don't know how to say this."

"Just say it," she told him firmly. "We've known each other a long time, Gary. Whatever it is, let's get it out in the open."

"All right—here goes! Marilyn, I've been very pleased with the arrangement we've had, and I'd very much like to move with your firm. But I'd rather have my office in the middle of a wheat field somewhere than next door to Luke Wilson—which is where you've put me." He saw the look on her face and spoke quickly, raising his hands to stop her from speaking. "No," he said, "Luke hasn't done anything wrong; he's always been terrific. I like the guy. But I tell you, Marilyn—I *cannot* work in an office where my clients and I have to listen to Luke's voice all the time. I'm a consultant; people come to my office expecting to sit and talk for hours. I'd be out of business in a month, if I lasted *that* long!"

"Oh . . . I see."

Marilyn nodded slowly. She did see; she knew exactly what he meant. Luke Wilson was a senior partner, and he brought in a lot of money for the firm; when Luke did cross-examination, people caved in with the speed of light. But his voice—the same voice that made him such a threat against the other side's witnesses in court—was terrible elsewhere. It was so nasal and so whining that it was like listening to a dentist's drill, and it was getting worse with every passing year.

"It really matters that much to you?" she asked Gary. "More than the location? More than the price? You know you can't do better than what we're offering—and we wouldn't offer it to anyone else, I assure you."

"It really matters that much," he said, "I'm sorry."

Does this scenario surprise you? It shouldn't! Read on.

Researching the Most Annoying American Voice

In 1993 I hired a leading independent research company to do a survey in which 1000 speakers of American English, both male and female, were asked the following question: "Which irritating or unpleasant voice annoys you the most?" Here are the results of that survey:

Voice Type	Percent Who Found It the Most Annoying
Whiny; complaining	44.0
High-pitched; squeaky	15.9
Loud and grating	12.1
Mumbling	11.1
Very fast talking	4.9
Weak and wimpy	3.6
Flat and monotonous	3.5
Heavy accent	2.4
Don't know; no response	2.6

Several things about these results deserve our notice. People responded with a number of different sorts of speech as candidates for the "Most Unwanted American Voice" title. They objected to voices that are too high, too loud, too weak, too accented, and more. But the runaway winner here is unmistakable: Almost half the people in the study were most annoyed by whiny, complaining voices. *That is: by voices with too much nasal quality.* Almost half! You couldn't ask for a more compelling reason to make absolutely certain that your own voice doesn't fit that description. A nasal whine is a real turn off, and what happened in the previous scenario is a typical example of the effects it can have and the havoc it can wreak in your life.

People base their judgment of your voice on two factors: its *quality*—that is, its tone, pitch, resonance, and nasality and other characteristics of sound—and *the way you use it.* They react to those items in combination, to arrive at a judgment of your voice as a whole, and to decide how they feel about it, and about *you*. Up to this point we've been focusing on the use of the voice; in this chapter we'll turn our attention to voice quality, starting with the problem of nasality.

Taking the Nasal Whine Out of Your Voice

When you talk, do you sound as if you're speaking through your nose? For the most part, speakers sound nasal when the muscles in the mouth, throat, and jaw become too tense and constricted. This keeps the sound from reaching lower resonance areas in the throat and chest, and most of the sound is directed into the nasal passages instead. When nasal sound goes on and on, a whining tone is the result.

Feeling sound vibrate in the nose as you speak does not necessarily mean that you sound nasal. Some people mistake nasal resonance for nasality. There is an important distinction between the two. Nasal resonance refers to sound vibrations produced in the nasal passages. This vibration or resonance adds ring and brightness to the voice and is a key ingredient in your overall sound. Nasality, on the other hand, is an *overconcentration* of sound in the nasal passages, resulting in a pinched and twangy tone.

Nasality can be corrected by learning to speak with a more open and relaxed mouth and throat. This will help to free the voice of any constriction.

RECOGNIZING THE TWO MOST COMMON NASAL SOUNDS

While extreme cases of nasality may affect the production of all vowels, the two sounds that are most often nasalized include the "ow" sound as in "now" and the short "a" sound as in "and."

Making the "OW" Sound

While words such as "count," "down," and "loud" are often nasalized in many parts of the country, speakers from the Northeastern and Southern states have a stronger tendency than others to twang this sound.

Before you can eliminate the nasality from the "ow" sound, you must first become aware of how it's produced. The "ow" sound is actually made up of two sounds: the "ah" sound as in "*father*" and the "oo" sound as in "*too*." (When these two sounds are joined together to form the "ow" sound, the result is called a *diphthong*.) Understanding how these two vowel sounds work together is a critical step in eliminating the nasal quality from this sound.

PRACTICE EXERCISE:　Follow these steps to produce the correct sound.

Step One: Say "AH"

Let your jaw drop down and open your mouth wide. Think of the mouth position you use when the doctor examines your throat. Make sure the mouth, throat, and jaw are all relaxed. Keep the tongue down. This sound needs a lot of room to travel freely. Repeat the "ah" sound. As you say "ah," concentrate on feeling vibrations in the throat and chest. These vibrations are signs of *resonance*. The more resonance you can feel in the throat and chest, the less nasal you will sound. Repeat the "ah" sound again.

Step Two: Join "AH" and "OO"

Begin by making the sound "oo" as in "too." Now make the "ah" sound followed by the "oo" sound. Say: "ah"—"oo." Now join the "ah" and the "oo" sound together without stopping the sound. Stress the "ah" sound and slowly say "ah—oo." To avoid sounding nasal you must begin with a very round and open-mouth position on the "ah" sound. Repeat the "ah—oo" sound.

PRACTICE EXERCISE: HOW

1. Using a round and open-mouth position, say "ah."
2. Stressing the "ah" sound, say "ah—oo."
3. Say the entire word slowly: "hah—oo" (h-o-w).

Repeat the sequence several times. Start out slowly, then gradually build up speed. Keep in mind that this new sound production may feel a bit strange at first. This is simply because the muscles in your mouth and throat are being used in a different way. That's why it's so important to practice slowly. You need the extra time to get a feel for this new sound production. Remember, to overcome any speech habit, you must go through a short period of readjustment. With time and regular practice, this will become second nature.

PRACTICE WORDS AND SENTENCES.   Use a very round and open-mouth position and keep the tongue down. Make sure the mouth, throat, and jaw are all relaxed. Concentrate on feeling vibration or resonance in the throat and chest areas. Be aware that there is a greater tendency to sound nasal when the nasal consonants *m* or *n* precede or follow the "ow" sound as in the words "*m*outh" and "pou*n*d."

amount	around	announce	abound
account	aloud	about	allow
arouse	brown	bound	boundary
bounce	bounty	blouse	bow
browse	bout	count	clown
crown	compound	confound	county
cloud	couch	crowd	coward
cower	down		

They were about to announce the amount.

Mr. Brown closed down the account.

Having no boundaries only compounded the problem.

drown	denounce	discount	doubt
devour	drowsy	drought	eyebrow
found	flounder	frown	fountain
founder	foul	flower	gown
gout	ground	growl	hound
hour	Howard	house	how

howl	impound	lounge	loud
loudspeaker	lousy		

Howard got a discount on the house.

I doubt if the founder is in the lounge.

How does the loudspeaker work by the fountain?

mound	mount	mountain	mouth
mouse	now	noun	ounce
owl	our	out	ouch
ousted	outline	outside	out loud
outcome	outbound	outfit	pounce
profound	pronounce	proud	pound
powder	power	powerhouse	pouch
prowl	round		

The pouch weighed two pounds and five ounces.

Turn the power on outside now.

We thought the outline was very profound.

rundown	roundabout	runaround	sound
surround	scrounge	scoundrel	south
shower	spouse	sour	scout
scour	scowl	slouch	spout
sprout	stout	town	tower
towel	trout	thousand	undoubtedly
voucher	vowel	vow	wow

The outbound calls were made from the south tower.

I like the sound of that town house.

They gave us the rundown on the voucher.

Making the Short "A" Sound

The short "a" sound as in "*ask*" is perhaps nasalized more than any other vowel sound. While the pinched and twangy short "a" sound can be heard throughout the country, words such as "half," "manager," and "answer" often take on an especially harsh quality in the upper Midwest region, including areas such as Chicago and Detroit. In fact, this extreme nasality is common among speakers as far east as New York.

PRACTICE EXERCISE: AS.   Getting the right pronunciation for the short "a" sound can be a little tricky. Take the word "as." If the muscles in the mouth and throat become too tense and constricted, the sound gets nasal. On the other hand, if you open the mouth and throat too wide, you can end up with a British pronunciation; that would be considered affected in American speech. To get the Standard American pronunciation for the short "a" sound, you need to strike a delicate balance between these two extremes. You can take the nasality out of "as" by following these three steps:

1. Open the mouth but don't let the lips pull back.
2. Relax the muscles in the mouth, throat, and jaw.
3. Keep the tongue down and say "as."

With the right mouth position, you should be able to feel a tiny amount of vibration or resonance in the throat and possibly chest. Remember, the more resonance you can feel in the throat and chest, the less nasal you will sound. Now repeat the exercise.

Keep in mind that there's a greater tendency to sound nasal when the nasal consonants *m* or *n* precede or follow the short "a" sound as in the words "*m*ath" and "ha*n*d."

PRACTICE WORDS AND SENTENCES.   Keep the tongue down and relax the mouth, throat, and jaw. Concentrate on feeling resonance in the throat and chest. Use a tape recorder to monitor your practice.

ask	bad	after	mass
had	add	half	staff
last	trap	path	basket

bashful	absolutely	wax	clash
pass	passage	habit	laugh
bag	baggage	fabric	matter
adequate	agony	flag	aspirin
snack	crash	apple	disaster
as	bathroom	master	class
math	cabin	gas	action
grab	cab	glass	vast
fraction	rational		

We only had half the staff.

I think the class action suit is irrational.

Your satisfaction is guaranteed when you buy this fabric.

Be aware that there is a greater tendency to nasalize the short "a" sound when it is followed by the nasal consonants "m," "n," and "ng." To avoid this, keep the back of the tongue down on the short "a" sound.

anthem	annual	amateur	ambulance
handle	and	Angela	ample
answer	amplifier	bland	banner
band	command	chance	candy
canyon	canned	Canada	camp
cantor	camera	can't	dancer
damp	Dan	frantic	France
Fran	family	fan	grand
gamble	Grammy	grant	ham
handsome	hand	Janet	

They played Canada's national anthem.

Dan had ample time to answer.

Janet handled the grant.

hamburger	anchor	hamper	janitor
jam	angle	lamp	land
bank	man	manner	mantle
manager	nasty	Nancy	pan
rank	pants	panting	ram
ran	ramp	handkerchief	random
blank	stamp	stand	sandwich
sank	snack	sand	strand
tangible	tantalize	rang	tan
trample	van	vandalize	tank
plan	drank	Andrew	thank
dangle	slang	Frank	

Randy's manager drafted the business plan.

Hank got angry when the phone rang.

Pam filled in the blanks.

SAYING COMMON PHRASES USING THE "OW" AND SHORT "A" SOUND

out of town	ask around
how about now	not bad
our last chance	no laughing matter
to grab a cab	after class
out of gas	there's no answer
have a ham sandwich	give a hand
in a jam	land a job
get panned	out of stamps
take a stand	master plan
hang up	rank and file
not allowed	clown around
down and out	lost and found

foul play	on the ground
pound for pound	hang around
down south	sweet and sour
out on the town	out and about
out to lunch	at a fraction of the cost

Keep in mind that nasality is a tough habit to break, so be patient when you practice.

Whenever you hear yourself sounding nasal and whiny in ordinary conversation, try to correct it right away. You'll find that it's going to require an increased level of awareness in order to catch yourself. Once you have the awareness, it's just a matter of making a subtle adjustment.

Getting Rid of Other Unwanted Voices to Improve Your Speech

Now let's go back to the survey and briefly consider some of the other voice problems listed there. The problem of "mumbling" was the subject of Chapter Two; Chapter Three took up the problem of speech that is too fast or too slow. Chapter Five will be devoted to the problems caused by heavy accents. That leaves a short list of four "unwanted voices" that we can summarize as too high; too monotonous; too loud and rough; too soft and weak.

These problems don't involve pronunciation; they are primarily matters of control and awareness. Chapters Six and Seven will deal with these issues in more detail. For now, here are a few things you can do to improve your voice if it has any of these characteristics.

LEARNING HOW TO BE AWARE OF YOUR VOICE

Everyone with normal hearing can learn to judge voices for all the qualities that we've been discussing. It's not hard to do, it's just something we get no training for and are not used to paying attention to. Hearing the characteristics of your *own* voice is hardest of all, because you are so accustomed to the way you sound. That's why putting your voice on tape is so useful—it helps you give your own voice the kind of attention you can give to the voices of other people.

Take the tape that you made at the beginning of this program, or one you've made since, and listen to it four times—once for pitch, once for loudness, once for strength, and once for monotonousness (or monotony's opposite, the "melodramatic" voice). Each time, ignore everything else about the tape and listen for just the one quality you're working on. Get someone else's opinion if you like; that's often helpful. Compare your taped voice with a tape made by someone else. Compare a tape you've made *recently* with the one you made first—you may be amazed at how much your voice has changed for the better.

Finally, use your common sense once again. If people back away from you when you talk to them, that's a clue—you are almost certainly talking too loud. If they frown and move closer to you, you're not talking loud enough. If their eyes glaze over as you speak, you're boring them; it may be because they find your voice monotonous. If they look startled, they may feel that your voice sounds melodramatic, with too much variation in pitch and rate and tone. The reactions that you get from those who are listening to you can be extremely helpful if you just remember to give them your attention. And you can test your skills by making the adjustments that you've learned from the voice control exercises and watching for changes in their reactions.

Certainly, voice quality shouldn't have so much power to affect what happens to you; as we've said before, it's not fair. But you don't have to put up with having one of the "most unwanted" voices and all its unjust consequences. This is something you can fix, using the information in this chapter.

LEARNING HOW TO CONTROL YOUR VOICE

For all four problems listed, you need to have better control of your voice, so that it does what you want it to do, when you want it done.

You need to know how your vocal muscles feel as you use them, so that you will have the skill needed to make deliberate adjustments and changes. Here are two traditional exercises that are used specifically for this purpose: *talking songs* and *talking trails.*

Using Talking Songs

For this exercise, choose a very simple song like "Three Blind Mice" or the chorus of "Jingle Bells." Then say the song out loud, changing the pitches just as if you were singing it—BUT DON'T SING! *Say* the tune instead of singing it. And as you do, pay very close attention to what your vocal muscles do to make the pitch go higher or lower. Begin by using just a nonsense syllable—"la, la, la"—instead of trying to pronounce the words, so that you can concentrate on the pitch. When you feel that you're comfortable with that, start saying the words, so that—as in many of the practice drills in earlier chapters— you learn how your vocal muscles *feel* while producing particular sounds. When you can do this with ease, move on to a more difficult song.

This exercise is one of the best—but it's hard to do, and it's not pretty. (You'll want to do it in private!) When you can do it well, there will be an automatic improvement in the quality of your voice because of your increased awareness of what you're doing with your vocal muscles and your increased ability to make deliberate changes.

Using Talking Trails

This is an easier exercise, and equally useful. Choose a paragraph from one of the brief speeches in the appendix to this book and read it aloud. (It's even better to memorize it so that you don't have to give your attention to reading it, if possible.) As you speak, imagine that as the sounds come out of your mouth they leave a trail in the air the way big jet planes leave contrails.

Your goal is to make the trails do what you want them to do. Make them go higher, go lower, stay absolutely flat, draw letters or shapes in the air . . . use your imagination. Again, pay close attention to what's happening in your mouth and throat and chest—your vocal tract—as you carry out particular moves.

If you find this is too difficult, start with "la, la, la" and work with that simple sound for a while—then move on to the speeches.

Matching a Taped Voice

Here's another useful strategy to help you gain better voice control. Talk *with* a tape by someone of your own gender and generation whose voice you admire. Don't listen and repeat; instead, talk simultaneously with the speaker on the tape and try to match that speaker's voice as naturally as you can. This often brings about very significant improvements in the pitch of your voice and in the speed at which you talk.

Say It Out Loud!

Here are four brief quotations that you can read aloud (and/or memorize to say aloud without reading) as a way to practice what you've learned in this chapter. Watch out for words that have a tendency to become nasal.

> *When he tried the hypermarket format in the late 1980s, Sam Walton simply grafted a grocery store onto a Wal-Mart store's general merchandise operation. It was like sewing a toe onto a hand.*
>
> ZINA MOUKHEIBER,
> "Squeezing the Tomatoes," *Forbes* Magazine, February 13, 1995, p. 55.

> *"Great strategy, lousy implementation." Ask the management consultants why their high-price recommendations sometimes produce rotten results, and that's the answer you'll get. Usually, the answer is merely self-serving. Sometimes it's dead right.*
>
> JOSEPH R. GARBER,
> "Being a Better Boss, the PC Way," *Forbes* Magazine, November 21, 1994, p. 206.

When outside forces make some types of assets more attractive than others, investors' reactions can unleash tidal waves of change, making or destroying fortunes. The most powerful of such outside forces is inflation.

JOHN RUTLEDGE,
"It's Back," *Forbes* Magazine, November 21, 1994, p. 50.

Ironically, some of the same academics who built giant reputations by slamming market timing are now making big bucks peddling a new variation of the same snake oil. The new product is called "tactical asset allocation" and is slickly packaged for respectability in complex computerese.

DAVID DREMAN,
"How to Avoid Whiplash," *Forbes* Magazine, October 1, 1990, p. 272.

5

Getting Rid of an Unfashionable Accent— A Roadblock to Success

HOW THE "WRONG" ACCENT CAN COST A PROMOTION

Ellen Hayes was on her way out, and she had planned to grab a quick hot dog on the street and spend the rest of her lunch hour doing some errands. But when she saw Dolores Ruiz crying at her desk, she canceled her plans.

"Come on, Dolores," she said briskly, "we're going to lunch! And not at some cafeteria, either—we're going to Halloran's where we can have a little privacy!"

"But I—"

"My treat!" Ellen added, and she hustled the other woman through the door and into the elevator, ignoring her objections. Only when they were safely in a back booth at Halloran's with two chef's salads and two coffees did she turn to Dolores and say, "All right, now, Dolores, let's have it! What's the matter? Why're you crying?"

"Oh, Ellen," Dolores answered, "I'm sorry to be such a mess—but I was *sure* they were going to let me have that administrative assistant's job this time! I was positive, you know? But they said exactly the same thing they said before. My English isn't good enough!"

"Hey . . . what's one promotion? There'll be lots more chances, right? And your English is getting better all the time. Really!"

Dolores looked down at her hands; they were shaking. "Ellen," she said, "wait till you hear who got the job."

"Who?"

"Marianne Dulaine."

Ellen's jaw dropped. "You're kidding me!"

"No. I'm not kidding. She got it."

"But she has a *much* heavier accent than you do!"

"Sure she does," said Dolores bitterly, stabbing a tomato wedge viciously with her fork. "But you see, Marianne has a *French* accent! That's different!"

Ellen stared at her friend, wondering what she could say to make her feel better. And then she had an idea.

"Dolores, I know exactly how you feel," she said seriously.

"No, you don't. You can't."

"I do, too," Ellen insisted. "You know why they didn't let me give the opening speech at the last sales meeting? The speech that I wrote, for crying out loud? It was because of my accent! The guys thought it would be bad for the company image. Okay?"

Now it was Dolores who was stunned. "No!" she said. "But you were *born* here! How could that happen?"

"Hey," Ellen told her, "listen, Dolores, you wanna be held back in this world? You just get yourself a Brooklyn accent like *I've* got, and see what happens to you!"

How Your Accent Affects Listeners

Do you have to struggle to make yourself understood because of a heavy accent? Does having even a slight accent make you feel a little uncomfortable when you speak? It comes as no surprise that an accent can become a communication barrier if it makes it difficult for others to understand you. Let's face it, in today's highly competitive business environment it's hard enough to grab and hold someone's attention even under the best of circumstances. If listeners must exert themselves just to make out what you're saying, that's already one big strike against you.

However, not all accents are viewed in the same way. Some accents can actually create a positive impression. For example, speaking with a French accent may be considered "cute" or romantic, while a British accent is often perceived as having a certain air of sophistication and refinement. There are other accents, however, such as the Spanish, Indian, and Asian varieties, that are often frowned upon. Why this is so may not be easy to answer, but nevertheless a certain prejudice docs exist. In fact, there have even been a few incidents of foreign-born Americans who have sued their employers over accent discrimination. One case involved an Indian-born employee who was dismissed from his job because his accent was "not good for the company's image." Another case featured a Cambodian-American bank employee who was passed over for promotion because of his accent.

You don't have to be a foreigner to run up against accent bias. Many American-born speakers with thick accents face regional prejudice even in their own country. As a top speech writer at a New York *Fortune* 500 company once admitted to me over lunch, "Don't ask me why, but every time I hear someone with a southern accent, I think the person's stupid." Other stereotypes exist as well. For example, the abrupt, fast-talking New Yorker is seen as rude, unfriendly, and abrasive. Likewise the flat, monotonous Mid-Westerner is perceived as bland and boring.

An accent also deserves attention if it makes the speaker feel uncomfortable, insecure, embarrassed, or self-conscious. A Spanish executive of a major international beverage company once approached his manager about getting some training to diminish his accent. His manager responded by saying, "Don't worry Carlos, you sound fine." Deep down Carlos felt his accent was undermining his confidence and eventually sought professional help on his own. Managers should bear in mind that accents are a highly sensitive issue. If someone comes to you for help, this in itself signals a major concern on the part of your employee. Also, if you ever need to suggest that an employee soften an accent, be as diplomatic as possible. Remember, accents are linked to a person's roots.

How to Tone Down Your Accent
to Change Your Image

Whether your accent is hurting your career or damaging your self-esteem, the good news is that you can do something about it. First, realize that losing your accent doesn't have to mean losing your identity. Completely eliminating your accent is not necessarily the goal. Gaining the ability to control it is far more important. The truth is, the world would be a very dull and boring place if we all sounded the same.

The exercises in this chapter are designed to help you tone down your accent to make your speech clearer and less distracting. The aim is to shoot for Standard American speech. This is the type of pronunciation that is most widely used and accepted by educated speakers across the country. It represents a generic speech pattern that is the easiest for everyone to understand. You know what it sounds like because Standard American English is used by the majority of radio and television announcers throughout the United States.

Whether it's an American accent, or a foreign accent, you'll learn to identify the key sounds that characterize your specific accent and make the necessary modifications to help diminish it.

Overcoming Your Regional Accent to
Break Down Communication Barriers

If you speak with a heavy accent you might sound "funny" to a lot of folks. In some cases you can even run the risk of alienating your listener. Imagine, if you will, a sales call between Jesse Jackson and Sylvester Stallone. A regional bias might well adversely affect their rapport and blow the sale. In general, when people with very different regional accents meet, it might take them longer to "warm up" to one another. This could pose a problem because in a real-life sales call every second counts. That's why it's a good idea to learn how to control your accent to adjust to the needs of each and every business situation.

The word "accent" refers to a type of pronunciation that is characteristic of a specific region or group. In the United States, some of the strongest accents can be heard in and around New York, Boston, and Chicago, as well as Texas and other southern states. Speakers from each of those regions all say their words a little differently. (Keep in mind that the accent traits outlined in this section do not necessarily apply to all speakers who live in a designated area of the country. The pronunciation differences that are listed are meant to represent the most typical speech patterns of a specific region.)

To make your speech clearer and less distracting you may need to make a few minor changes in how you pronounce certain key sounds. But don't worry, this won't make your speech come across as phony or affected. Changing a few sounds isn't going to make you talk like Henry Higgins in *My Fair Lady*. You're simply aiming to knock out some of the biggest problems and move toward "standard" pronunciation of American English or something close to it.

Every effort has been made here to spell out sounds in the easiest way possible. No confusing pronunciation symbols are used, just the plain old letters of the alphabet.

LOSING YOUR NEW YORK ACCENT

The famous New York accent—the one comedians make fun of with lines like "The goil saw a boid"—is instantly recognizable. This dialect is not limited to Brooklyn, or even to New York, although it is used primarily by urban Americans. Its speakers vary widely in the number and degree of deviations from Standard American English that they use. The New York accent does not cover the "entire range of northeastern varieties of English." The Boston and Philadelphia accents are quite different from the New York accent.

Many people believe that New Yorkers just don't enunciate well. Actually, much of the time, it's just the opposite. People from this region tend to overenunciate their words. Their mouth movements are usually so forceful that it almost sounds as if some speakers are "punching out" their words. Just think of the way Sylvester Stallone talked in the movie *Rocky* or how Archie Bunker spoke in "All in the Family."

Handling Specific New York Problem Sounds

Many of the sound differences that are typical of this accent (for example, dropping final consonants and substituting "d" for "th") have already been covered thoroughly in Chapter Two of this book. If you have a New York accent, you will want to give plenty of time to the exercises and drills in that chapter. We will concentrate here on other features of the dialect that cause problems. As you work with the exercises below, I recommend listening frequently to a recording of a Standard American English speaker, to help you hear the standard pronunciation of the troublesome sounds; a tape of the evening news, with Peter Jennings or Diane Sawyer as anchorperson, is a good choice.

What to Do When "Talk" Sounds Like "tAWWK"

(I've used oversized letters to illustrate just how much a heavy-duty New Yorker would overdo this vowel sound.)

The "aw" sound is much too heavy. The lips are too round and tense and the sound is made too far forward in the mouth. Don't pucker your lips; instead, relax the lips and jaw. Feel the "aw" sound coming from farther back in the mouth. Concentrate on lightening up your "aw" sound as you do the exercises.

PRACTICE WORDS AND SENTENCES

applause	glossy	ought	coffee
because	across	bought	wrong
loft	hall	loss	author
taught	walk	thought	boss
water	cause	office	toward
awful	false	flaw	August
cost	broad	launch	

The project was launched in August.

There's strong talk of a walkout.

Cuts were made across the board.

What to Do When "Choice" Sounds Like "chOOYYce"

Here's another example of a vowel sound that's overdone. If your "aw" sound is too heavy, chances are your "oi" sound will need to be lightened up a bit as well. Remember, overemphasizing certain sounds can create a negative impression. This "oy" sound is overemphasized as well. Again, the lips are too round and tense and the sound is made too far forward in the mouth.

Don't pucker your lips, instead relax the lips and jaw. Feel the "oy" sound coming from farther back in the mouth. Ease up on the "oy" sound as you say the following practice words and sentences:

PRACTICE WORDS AND SENTENCES

choice	joint	spoil	exploit
voice	poignant	enjoy	void
oil	soil	employment	coin
royal	appointment	point	rejoice
join	loyal	poise	foyer
avoid	voyage	toilet	destroy

Roy made a poignant suggestion.

There's high unemployment in Troy.

You have a choice of appointments.

What to Do When "Tie" Sounds Like "Toy"

A chiropractor from New Jersey came to me with what I like to call a "spine" problem. We both agreed he was in need of a sound adjustment. Whenever he said "spine," it sounded more like "spoin." He realized that his strong regional accent eroded his authority and wasn't helping his practice. The problem with this pronunciation is that the lips are pushed slightly forward and the mouth opening is too narrow.

To correct this, open the mouth wide and say "ah," the way you would when the doctor examines your throat. Add the "ee" sound as in "fee" and say "ah—ee." Join the "ah" and "ee" together and say "*ah*ee." Stress the "ah" sound. Using the same "*ah*ee" sound, say the word "spine" (sp-*ah*-een).

PRACTICE WORDS AND SENTENCES.   Try out the new "i" sound in the following words and sentences:

type	price	advice	guide
private	satisfy	aisle	title
resign	imply	twice	right
sign	design	strike	high-rise
society	arrive	trial	
describe	climate	rely	
file	sideline	decide	

My flight never arrives on time.

Is that title on file?

Think twice before resigning.

What to Do When "Straight" Sounds Like "Shtraight"

Some New Yorkers substitute "sh" for "s" in "str" words. This is just another example of speech that signals a lack of polish to your listener. The problem is that the lips push forward forming a "sh" sound.

Take away the initial "s" sound and say "trait." Now add on the "s" and say "ss—trait." Make sure you are pulling the lips back slightly to make a clean, hissing "s" sound. Now slowly join the "s" together with "trait" and say "*str*aight." If you hear the "sh" sound creeping in again, it means your lips are pushing forward.

PRACTICE WORDS AND SENTENCES.   Aim for a clear "str" sound in these practice words and sentences.

street	strict	strike	strive
strong	strengthen	stringent	structure
struggle	strategy	strenuous	abstract
construct	destroy	distract	instruct
restrict	administration		

The labor strike was very stressful.

Give us a straightforward answer on the strategy.

It was a struggle for this administration.

What to Do When "Bird" Sounds Like "Boyd"

This is the pronunciation difference that people associate most closely with a New York accent; it's one you really don't want to have in your speech. Not because it is "wrong" or "an error," but because the negative reaction to it in listeners is so widespread and so intense that it interferes with your ability to communicate effectively. Even though this pronunciation difference is less widespread today, it still can be heard from time to time and deserves a mention here.

Fortunately, this problem is easily solved. Imagine that it's a bitterly cold day and you're standing out on the sidewalk wearing only your bathing suit. Your most probable comment is "Brrrrrrr," right? To make the change you need to give "bird" the Standard English pronunciation, just say "Brrrrrrrr" and add the final "d." Say "brrrrrrrrd"; there you are! And for each of the practice words and sentences, follow the same strategy, using the "rrrr" instead of the "oy" of your dialect.

Practice Words and Sentences

bird	third	word	heard
girl	journey	curve	turn
curb	serve	hurt	germ

I heard the girl say a six-syllable word.

A desperate country may turn to germ warfare.

The worst part of the journey was the third week.

LOSING YOUR SOUTHERN ACCENT

As was true for the discussion of the New York accent, many of the pronunciation problems of southern speakers have been covered in earlier sections of this book. They won't be repeated here; instead we will focus on other items that cause southern speakers trouble.

Handling Specific Southern Speech Problems

When you think of a southern accent, perhaps one of the first things that comes to mind is how the words get drawn out. Just think for a moment about how Jimmy Carter talks. For many people unfamiliar with southern accents, there are times when we can't even understand what he's saying. Southerners also speak with a distinctive amount of lilt, or pitch change. Take the phrase, "It was a *disaster*." A person with a heavy southern accent might say this like:

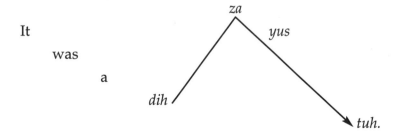

Notice how "disaster" really gets drawn out, and how the pitch glides way up and down. This elongation and gliding effect is what gives the southern accent its unique flavor.

So, to soften your accent, you need to cut down on the number and frequency of changes in pitch, and the amount of *time* you give to your vowels. Of course, in order not to sound monotonous, you still have to modulate the voice as you speak. The main point is, you don't want your vowel sounds to get *too* springy.

As far as overall voice quality is concerned, many southerners tend to speak with somewhat of a high-pitched, nasal twang. (Just think of Senator Phil Gramm.) People from the South also tend to speak with a very closed mouth, which may cause words to sound slurred. Learning to open up a bit wider will help you speak more clearly and distinctly. You'll also sound a lot less nasal and whiny.

Look over the following list of pronunciation differences and see which sound you need to modify to soften your southern accent.

What to Do When "Class" Sounds Like "Claayus"

Adding an extra "ya" sound to the vowel creates the lilt and drawl. The "a" sound is pinched and nasalized, and one word sounds as if it has two syllables instead of one.

Take out the extra "ya" sound and say "class." Keep the vowel sound short and don't glide down in pitch. Open the mouth a little wider and keep the tongue down to avoid a nasal twang.

PRACTICE WORDS AND SENTENCES

ask	staff	France	glass
answer	chance	manager	last
flag	handle	land	
after	grant	master	
half	plan	stamp	

This is your last chance to take action.

The flag is at half-mast.

Ask the manager for some stamps.

For additional exercises on this sound see Chapter Four.

What to Do When "Taught" Sounds Like "Taw-wuht"

Adding the extra "wuh" sound to the vowel creates the lilt and drawl. The lips become too round and the mouth position is too narrow on the vowel sound.

Take out the extra "wuh" sound and say "tawt." Make the vowel sound short and avoid gliding down in pitch. Keep the mouth wide open on the "aw" sound and feel the sound coming from farther back in the mouth.

PRACTICE WORDS AND SENTENCES

office	boss	because	law
toward	stall	wrong	across
applause	August	awful	loss
talk	glossy	cost	cause
thought	off	strong	mall
broad	false	author	draw
launch	flaw	vault	
loft	bought	sought	

I thought of all the wrong things.

Paul's office is across the hall.

It's set to launch in August.

What to Do When "Type" Sounds Like "Top"

Many southerners shorten this vowel sound. Instead of making a long "i" sound, as in the letter "i" of the alphabet, they make a short "ah" sound.

Open the mouth wide and say "ah." Add the long "ee" sound as in "see" and say "ah—ee." Join the two sounds together and say "*ah*ee." Stress the "ah" sound. Using the same "*ah*ee" sound, say the word "type" ("t*ah*eep").

PRACTICE WORDS AND SENTENCES

deny	side	high-rise	twice
resign	private	rely	decide
society	science	item	satisfy
advice	sideline	describe	sign
collide	guide	price	arrive
design	file	trial	
title	identify	China	
apply	aisle	strike	

Now is the time to decide.

Who designed that high-rise?

My advice is to buy it Friday.

What to Do When "Joy" Sounds Like "Jaw"

The "oy" sound is another vowel sound that southerners tend to cut too short. Instead of making a long "oy" sound, they substitute a short "aw" sound.

Say "aw" as in "*aw*ful." Add the long "ee" sound as in "fee" and say "aw—ee." Join the two sounds together and say "*aw*ee." Stress the "aw" sound. Using the same "*aw*ee" sound, say the word "joy" ("j*aw*ee").

PRACTICE WORDS AND SENTENCES

employ	destroy	oil	choice
void	turmoil	avoid	voice
spoil	poignant	appointment	point
royal	oyster	joint	
loyal	foyer	exploit	

Lloyd enjoyed the voyage.

Try to avoid making too much noise.

Please join us in the foyer.

What to Do When "Pen" Sounds Like "Pin"

A priest from the South had the hardest time getting the Standard American pronunciation for the number 10. In his sermons, every time he wanted to say "The Ten Commandments" it came out sounding more like "The *Tin* Commandments."

Many southerners (as well as some Mid-Westerners) tend to turn the short "e" sound into the short "i" sound. This happens most often when short "e" is followed by "m" and "n" as in "stem" and "end."

Open the mouth and throat a little wider as you make the short "e" sound. Feel the sound coming from slightly farther back in the mouth. Keep in mind that the difference between "pen" and "pin" is a very subtle one. You may need to have someone who can differentiate between these two sounds listen to you practice and provide some feedback.

PRACTICE WORDS AND SENTENCES.   Differentiate between the following short "i" and short "e" sounds.

Short "i"	*Short "e"*
been	Ben
gym	gem
him	hem
mini	many
since	sense
tin	ten
tint	tent
win	when
windy	Wendy

Send plenty of pens.

Ten men were members.

The chemist has tenure.

What to Do When "Town" Sounds Like "tAyAown"

A southern executive came to me because she wanted to get rid of the twang in her speech. When she listened to the sound of her voice on her telephone answering machine, she heard, "I'm not in right *na-yaow.*

The "ow" sound is drawled and nasalized. The lips are pulled back and tense and the mouth opening is too narrow. The word sounds as if it had two syllables.

Open the mouth wide and say "ah." Add the "oo" sound as in "too" and say "*ah*—oo." Join the two sounds together and say "*ah*oo." Stress the "ah" sound. Using the same "*ah*oo" sound, say the word "town" ("*ta*hoon"). Keep the tongue down and feel the sound coming from farther back in the mouth.

PRACTICE WORDS AND SENTENCES

now	aloud	outline	profound
account	founder	down	ounce
gown	boundary	surround	
towel	voucher	fountain	
sound	house	south	

The founder closed the account.

Now you can sign the voucher.

There's a towel by the shower.

Additional drills for this sound can be found in Chapter Four.

How to Stop Cutting Words Short

Many southerners shorten the long vowel sounds that, in Standard English, end certain words. For example, make a long vowel sound at the end of words like "fellow," "value," and "country."

For "fellow," don't say: "fell-*uh*," say: "fell-*oh*."

For "value," don't say: "val-*yuh*," say: "val-*yoo*."

For "country," don't say: "kun-tr*ih*," say: "kun-t*ree*."

How to Stop Stressing the Wrong Syllable of a Word

Many southerners incorrectly stress the first syllable of certain words. For instance, stress the second syllable in words like "umbrella," "entire," "police," and so on.

For "umbrella," don't say: "úm-brel-uh," say: "um-brél-uh."

For "entire," don't say: "én-tire," say: "en-tíre."

For "police," don't say: "póh-lees," say: "puh-lées."

For "Detroit," don't say: "Dé-troit," say: "De-tróit."

How to Stop Slurring Words

As a rule, southerners tend to be a little too relaxed when it comes to enunciating their words. This affects both consonants and syllables. For example, "t" and "d" endings are often dropped so "draft" may become "draf" and "find" may become "fine." A three-syllable word such as "company" (kum-puh-nee) may lose a syllable and become "kump-nih." Also, many southerners have a habit of slurring words, so the phrase "What are you doing?" may sound more like "Whatcha doin?" (A complete listing of enunciation drills is given in Chapter Two.)

As you work on toning down your accent, remember that the ultimate goal is to make your speech as easy as possible for everyone to understand. You're not really losing anything, you're simply gaining the ability to control your accent. This means you no longer will have to feel uncomfortable or self-conscious about how you sound. You'll see that changing just a few key sounds can really make a dramatic difference. With a little bit of practice you'll speak with greater clarity and confidence, projecting a more polished and professional image.

Say It Out Loud!

Here are four brief quotations that you can read aloud (and/or memorize to say aloud without reading) as a way to practice what you've learned about how to tone down your accent. Aim for a "standard" pronunciation of American English.

> *It costs roughly five times more to get a new customer than to keep a current one. So the loyal customers are the ones who generate the profits.*
>
> JOSHUA LEVINE,
> "Relationship Marketing," *Forbes* Magazine, December 20, 1993,
> p. 233.

> *What Conrail needs more than anything is longer hauls, because that's where the money is made in railroading. As part of a bigger system or systems, Conrail would be immensely valuable. On its own, it will always be chugging uphill.*
>
> JAMES R. NORMAN,
> "Choose Your Partners!," *Forbes* Magazine, November 21, 1994, p. 89.

> *No matter how skilled a player you are in business, at some point you're going to find yourself on defense . . . . Remember what the coaches say: "You can't score on defense. Get the ball."*
>
> ROGER AILES,
> "Scoring on Defense: Tactics to Defeat the Hostile Questioner,"
> *Success,* December 1988, p. 14.

*One thing you quickly learn from corporate autobiographies is
that people don't become CEOs by accident. While you and I
are traipsing mindlessly through life, these brilliant men with
steel-trap minds are constantly learning, absorbing, filing away
information for that day when it can be used to good advantage.
Everything they do in life is a lesson.*

> JOSEPH NOCERA,
> "Iacocca-Heads: What's Wrong with Business Books,"
> *The New Republic,* March 2, 1987, p. 32.

Modifying Your Foreign Accent to Make Yourself Understood

Foreigners face a particularly tough time when trying to master the pronunciation of Standard American English. For one thing, very often there
seems to be little or no correlation between the way a word is spelled
and how it is pronounced. For example, "iron" is pronounced "i-urn,"
"colonel" is pronounced "kúr-nel," "ocean" is pronounced "óh-shun,"
"bury" is pronounced "bér-ee," and so on. Then there are the words
spelled with "ough" like "en*ough*," "thr*ough*," "alth*ough*," and "pl*ough*"
that are all pronounced differently. It's enough to drive a person crazy!

To make matters worse, there are some sounds in English, such
as the "th" sound as in "*th*in," that are rare in other languages. This
means that as a foreigner, the muscles in your mouth are not accustomed to forming certain sounds and must be trained from scratch.

Also, when you studied English in your native country most of the
focus probably was placed on grammar and vocabulary. How you said
a word was usually less important. As a result, some of the more subtle pronunciation differences may not have been taught at all.

The exercises given here will help you master some of the most
troublesome vowel and consonant sounds in English. But before you
can really become a convincing speaker, you need to perfect one other
very important skill: how to stress your words. Learning the changing
patterns of stress will not only make you easier to understand but will
definitely make you more interesting to listen to as well.

STRESSING THE RIGHT SYLLABLES TO IMPROVE YOUR ENGLISH

No matter how accurately you pronounce your vowels and consonants, you can still throw off your listener by stressing or accenting the wrong part of a word. You certainly wouldn't want to tell someone that you're doing business in the *forest* when you mean the *Far East!* Just the slightest shift in stress can change a word and completely alter the meaning of your statement. Imagine how confused things could get if you said you had to go to the *personal* department when you really meant the *personnel* department. Or think what could happen if you told a salesperson that you wanted to *differ* payments when you really meant to say *defer* payments. As odd as they may sound, the above are just some of the many stress mistakes foreigners make all the time.

Differentiating Between Strong and Weak Beats

In some languages the syllables of a word are given equal amounts of stress or emphasis. Not so in English. All words with two or more syllables have strong and weak beats. Strong beats occur on stressed syllables. Weak beats occur on unstressed syllables. For example, notice the difference in stress on the noun "convert" and the verb "convert." In the verb, a weak syllable is followed by a strong syllable. In the noun "convert" (káhn-vert), a strong syllable is followed by a weak syllable. Foreigners also often don't make *enough* of a contrast between strong and weak syllables. If it's unclear which syllable you're trying to stress, your listener may easily misunderstand you. A French executive once told me that she was going to *Indiana police*. She meant to say *Indianapolis* but didn't know how to stress the word correctly.

One very good tip is to listen carefully to how native speakers stress their words in ordinary conversation or on the TV or radio. If you hear a different syllable being stressed than what you're used to, chances are they're right and you're wrong. So keep a pocket-sized notebook or some small index cards handy to jot down new stress patterns that you may come across during the course of a day.

Bear in mind that this whole issue of strong and weak stress can seem quite overwhelming at first. Just remember that awareness is the first crucial step. Once your ear becomes attuned to the changing patterns of stress, you'll be amazed at how quickly you can incorporate these new patterns into your everyday speech.

CHANGING PITCH FOR EMPHASIS

Remember that the stressed syllable is the most important part of a word so it needs to be hammered out with a great deal of force. In contrast, the unstressed syllable is not important and gets no emphasis whatsoever. But it's not just a matter of loud and soft. In a stressed syllable, the vowel sound is also higher in pitch and a little longer than in an unstressed syllable. For example, in a four-syllable word such as "communicate," the stress pattern would look something like this:

M-E-W
                              nih
        kuh   kate

Notice how the pitch shoots way up on the stressed syllable "mew" and then comes down in small steps on the remaining two unstressed syllables. This up-and-down pitch pattern is one of the most important ways to create emphasis. However, many foreigners are not accustomed to using a lot of pitch variation in their speech. In fact, if you listen to a tape recording of your own speech, you may be surprised just how flat and monotonous you sound compared with American-born speakers. As one of my Russian students commented after hearing himself on tape, "My God, I sound like a robot!" A sure-fire way to put your audience to sleep. So to make your speech clearer and more interesting to listen to, you really need to exaggerate the amount of pitch change at first, especially on the stressed syllables.

Remember, stressing words and syllables is not a subtle matter. If you play it too safe and hit each syllable with the same amount of force, you may confuse your listener. On the other hand, you will remember from reading the section on unfashionable American accents that southern speakers have to learn not to put too *much* stress on syllables. You want just enough to make it clear that the syllable is stressed, but not so much that listeners perceive your speech as "melodramatic."

The best way to get this right, frankly, is to practice with a recording of an American English speaker. This is especially true if your native language is a tone language (like Mandarin Chinese or Navajo or Thai). The pitch changes that go with English stress, unlike the pitch changes that go with tones, do not ordinarily change the meaning of the word. (The noun/verb "convert/convert" pair is one of the few exceptions; that's why it's used as an example.)

Recognizing the Right Syllable to Stress

It would be nice if I could just give you a small set of rules that would always tell you which syllable of an English word to stress. I can't; the few rules available are written by linguists and are far too complicated for our purposes. The basic facts are:

- Every English word with more than one syllable has to stress one syllable more than the other(s).

- Some English words have even more stresses, giving one syllable *primary* stress (the strongest) and others *secondary* or *tertiary* stresses (not as strong as primary, but stronger than for an unstressed syllable).

- English punctuation doesn't provide any clue (like an accent mark) to tell you where to put the stresses.

So, now that you know how important stress is, how do you know where to put it?

You don't ordinarily need to concern yourself about trying to add subtle degrees of stress. Just get the primary stress right, pay attention to the English pronunciation used by native speakers, and the nonprimary stresses will take care of themselves.

Using a Dictionary

A good dictionary is your best bet. Make sure your dictionary has a pronunciation guide next to each word. If yours doesn't, go out and buy one that does. It may be one of the best investments you'll ever make! Be aware that stress marks may be written differently in some editions. For example, one dictionary may place the stress mark *before* the *first* letter of the stressed syllable in "locate" as in `loh-kate, while another may have the stress mark *after* the *last* letter of the stressed syllable as in loh´-kate. Either way, syllables are always separated by dots or dashes so you'll always know which part of the word to emphasize.

In addition to a dictionary for the home, I recommend a vest-pocket dictionary (with pronunciation guides) to all my foreign students. Its compact size lets you take it along wherever you go. You'll have a great companion when you're in a jam.

EIGHT GUIDELINES TO DETERMINE WHICH SYLLABLES TO STRESS

While it's true that English grammar doesn't provide hard and fast rules to determine which part of a word should be stressed, there are a few guidelines that can help. Here are some pointers worth remembering. Keep in mind that these are just guidelines; some of them have exceptions.

1. When a noun ends in "tion," stress the syllable before the "tion" ending. Examples:

locátion	solútion	petítion	imitátion
resolútion	imaginátion	globalizátion	communicátion

2. When a noun ends in "ity," stress the syllable before the "ity" ending. Examples:

abílity	capabílity	availabílity	responsibílity
personálity	insánity	reálity	

3. When an adjective ends in "ical," stress the syllable before the "ical" ending. Examples:

   polítical   rádical   práctical   analýtical
   económical   psychológical

4. When an adjective ends in "ic," stress the syllable before the "ic" ending. Examples:

   fantástic   realístic   futurístic   democrátic
   optimístic   económic

5. When an adjective ends in "ial" or "ual," stress the syllable before the "ial" or "ual" ending. Examples:

   ánnual   mútual   púnctual   fináncial
   indústrial   controvérsial   unúsual   indivídual
   intelléctual   editórial

6. When a verb ends in "ify," stress the syllable before the "ify" ending. Examples:

   rátify   idéntify   clárify   símplify
   módify   spécify   quálify

7. In a compound noun (a noun consisting of more than one word), stress the syllables that would normally be stressed in each word but stress the first word harder than the second. Examples:

   stock broker   *music* director
   health care   *police* department
   share holders   *press* release

8. In capital letter abbreviations, stress the last letter. Examples:

   I.D́.   U.Ś.   F.B.Í.
   USÁ   FDIĆ   SEĆ
   IRŚ   CEÓ   CIÁ

Here are some examples of shifting stress patterns. Notice how the stress of a syllable can shift depending on the form of a word:

pólitics	political	politícian
démocrat	demócracy	democrátic
analýtical	ánalyze	análysis
confíde	confidéntial	confidentiálity

LEARNING TO PRONOUNCE COMMON WORDS THAT CAN GIVE YOU TROUBLE

Review this list and improve your batting average!

álternate	rétailing	curtáiling
próceeds (noun)	enginéering	propríetary
ínventory	méchanism	éxecute
exécutive	stábilize	strátegy
stratégic	décade	óriented
órigin	índicate	spécify
specífic	prióriy	contráctual
áctivism	ínfluence	influéntial
córporate	cómparable	óperating
ínstinct	distínct	sevérely
cátegory	categórically	excél
efféct	éfficacy	régulatory
trustée	íntrigue (noun)	próspect
prospéctus	cónstitutes	constítuency
súbsidy	subsídiary	désignate
expertíse	législative	offícial
áuthorize	authórity	ínterview

intervéne	súbsidy	subsídiary
annúity	éxcess	succéss
dívidend	símulate	cólleague
nécessary	necéssity	délicacy
cómpetent	ínventory	

If you're getting all stressed out, take a break. Remember, when in doubt, consult your dictionary.

Sentences to Use in Practicing Your New Skills

Now it's time to try out your new stress skills in some sentences. Make sure that you are using a lot of pitch variation. You might want to tape record yourself or have someone else monitor you. Remember, the biggest pitch change comes on the stressed syllable of a word. Not only will this make you easier to understand, it will give your speech more variety and make you a much more interesting speaker:

The entrepreneur introduced many innovative ideas.

We were involved in an intricate controversy.

They pursued a diverse group of proprietary computers.

Some executives severely curtailed their expenses.

All proceeds went into the retailing business.

CORRECTING VOWEL SOUNDS TO IMPROVE YOUR SPEECH

Many non-native speakers of English have trouble distinguishing among certain groups of vowel sounds. For example, say the following sentence out loud: "What *color* was the *caller's collar*?" Do "color," "caller," and "collar" all sound the same? If you answered "yes" then you're not alone. The fact remains, however, that all three words should be pronounced differently. If *you're* confused about what the difference is, just imagine how confused your listener is going to be! Fortunately, there are some guidelines that can help. There are three ·key questions you should always ask yourself when comparing and contrasting vowel sounds.

1. Is the vowel pronounced with tense muscles (like the word "I") or with relaxed ones (like the "i" in "Bill")?

2. Is the vowel sound made with a wide open or partially closed mouth position?

3. Is your tongue positioned towards the front, middle, or back of your mouth?

Keep in mind that many times foreigners make the tense vowel sounds too short and the lax vowel sounds too long. Also, most non-native speakers don't open the mouth wide enough on the more open vowel sounds.

SPECIFIC VOWEL PROBLEMS TO RESOLVE

Certain pairs of vowel sounds are especially troublesome. Take a look at the word groups that follow and see which ones you really need to work on.

Saying Long "EE" and Short "I" Correctly: "Reach" vs. "Rich"

What's the difference?

The "ee" sound in *reach* is a tense (often referred to as "long") vowel sound, as in the letter "e" of the alphabet. The lips are pulled back slightly in a smile-like position. The tongue is positioned towards the front of the mouth. The "i" sound in *rich* is a lax (often referred to as "short") vowel sound. The lips are slightly parted and relaxed. The tongue is positioned towards the front of the mouth.

Here is a list of words for practicing this contrast. Read each word aloud from left to right. Make sure you can hear and feel the difference in the tense and lax vowel sounds.

Tense "EE" (Long)	*Lax "I" (Short)*
steal	still
heat	hit
leave	live (verb)
peak	pick
read (present tense)	rid
feel	fill
seat	sit
least	list
peel	pill
seek	sick

AVOIDING EMBARRASSING MISTAKES.   Want to know what can happen if you make the long "ee" sound too short? Imagine politely asking a stranger, "Which way is the *bitch*?" instead of "Which way is the *beach*?" Once, a student of mine tried to tell me, "I need a sh*eet* of paper." Unfortunately, the long "ee" sounded more like the short "i" as in "hit." When I asked her to repeat herself, she realized her mistake and her face turned as red as a tomato.

PRACTICE WORDS AND SENTENCES

Long (Tense) "EE"

team	unique	equal	veto
east	speak	achieve	field
evening	receipt	chief	relief
complete			

Short (Lax) "I"

industry	business	signature	building
interim	bill	interest	income
assistant	skill	instill	
system	dividend	busy	

He needs the signatures of all three women.

The building industry is in the East.

She makes frequent business trips.

Saying Long "AY" and Short "E" Correctly: "Taste" vs. "Test"

What's the difference?

The "ay" sound in *taste* is a long vowel sound as in the letter "a" of the alphabet. The long "ay" sound is formed by gliding from the "eh" sound as in "set" to the "ee" sound in "seat" as in "eh—ee." The "eh" sound is stressed. So "taste" would look something like "*teh*-eest." The lips should be pulled back slightly and the tongue positioned towards the front of the mouth. The "e" sound in *test* is a short vowel sound. There is no gliding effect. The lips are relaxed and the tongue is positioned towards the front of the mouth.

Practice these contrasting sounds and you'll soon get the hang of it. Read each word aloud from left to right.

Long (Tense) "AY"	*Short (Lax) "E"*
gate	get
saint	sent
waste	west
main	men
sale	sell
pain	pen
aid	Ed
age	edge
late	let
wait	wet

Just the slightest change can completely alter the meaning. What if, for example, a member of a special business task force announced to the group that they needed to rethink the "*debt* issue" when what he really meant was take a look at the "*date*"?

PRACTICE WORDS

Long (Tense) "AY"

major	raise	mail	mistake
aim	freight	weigh	eight
straight	failure	April	complain
payday	waiter	labor	vacant

Short (Lax) "E"

president	measure	ready	again*
says	said	any	breakfast
deadline	spread	many	friend
threaten	pleasant	head	bread

*In American English, "again" is pronounced "uh-*gen*."

The president made a fatal mistake.

Our aim is to have a pleasant stay.

We failed to meet the deadline again.

Saying "OH" and "AW" Correctly: "Low" vs. "Law"

What's the difference?

The "oh" sound in *low* is a long vowel sound as in the letter "o" of the alphabet. It is formed by gliding from the "uh" sound in "c*u*t" to the "oo" sound in "*zoo*" as in "uh—oo." The "uh" sound is stressed. So "low" would look something like "*luh*-oo." The lips should be rounded and the tongue is positioned towards the back of the mouth.

The "aw" sound in *law* is a short vowel sound. There is no gliding effect. The lips move forward slightly and the tongue is positioned towards the back of the mouth.

Practice these contrasting sounds and read each word aloud from left to right.

Long (Tense) "OH"	*Short (Lax) "AW"*
coal	call
choke	chalk
toll	tall
boat	bought
woke	walk
goes	gauze
row	raw
owe	awe
oat	ought
stole	stall

When I asked a student of mine what nationality she was, she proudly answered, "I'm paw-lish." As it turned out, her "oh" sound could have used a bit more polish. Naturally, she meant to say *Polish*.

You want to make a clear distinction between the vowel sounds in "won't" and "want." Since these words have very different meanings, they can easily create a problem if you don't pronounce them just right. Just imagine the trouble you could get into if your manager thought you said "I *won't* go to the seminar" when you actually meant to say "I *want to* go to the seminar." To make a clear contrast, here's a good practice sentence to try: "You *won't want* to miss this."

Practice Words and Sentences

Long (Tense) "OH" Sound

don't	won't	sew	local
open	moment	total	motivate
motion	photo	hello	know

| loan | phone | toast | postpone |
| enclose | notice | proposal | |

Short (Lax) "AW" Sound

launch	August	boss	cost
salt	fault	pause	thought
bought	caught	office	hallway
applaud	coffee	auto	author

Watch out for tricky spellings. When some foreigners see a word spelled with "au" they make an "ow" sound as in "town" or an "oh" sound as in "go." A student once said to me, "My company is going to *low*nch a new product." At first, I thought he said "lunch" or "lounge." Then I realized he meant to say "launch."

Contrast the "oh" and "aw" sounds in the following sentences:

The post office was closed in August.

Send the proposal to my boss.

What is the total cost of the phone?

Saying "OO" and "UU" Correctly: "Pool" vs. "Pull"

What's the difference?

The "oo" sound in *pool* is a long vowel sound. The lips are very rounded and somewhat tense. The tongue is positioned toward the back of the mouth.

The "uu" sound in *pull* is a short vowel sound. The lips are very relaxed and not rounded. The tongue is positioned toward the back of the mouth.

Many speakers from the Eastern European countries, especially Russia, have a habit of rounding and tensing the lips on the short "uu" sound so "*look* at the *book*" sounds more like "*luke* at the *buke*."

See how well you can contrast these sounds.

Long (Tense) "OO"	*Short (Lax) "UU"*
fool	full
Luke	look
who'd	hood
stewed	stood
food	foot
wooed	wood

One of the reasons these two vowel sounds are so confusing is that very often they have the same "oo" or "u" spelling but are pronounced differently. For example, "fool" has a long vowel sound while "wool" has a short vowel sound.

PRACTICE WORDS AND SENTENCES

Long (Tense) "OO"

lose	fewer	jewel	suit
dual	duty	fluency	June
pseudo	studio	fruit	through
include	Cuba	conclusion	group
coupon	improving	annuity	

Short (Lax) "UU"

could	would	should	good
took	hook	shook	woman
push	sugar	rookie	
bullet	cushion	understood	
wool	boulevard	crooked	

Try to hear and feel the difference when saying the "oo" and "uu" sounds in the following sentences:

Only Louis understood the annuity plan.

The woman forgot to include the booklet.

The group couldn't reach any conclusion.

Differentiating Between Sounds Like: *"Collar" vs. "Color"*

What's the difference?

The "ah" sound in *collar* is a long vowel sound. It's the same "ah-h-h-h" sound you make when the doctor examines your throat. The mouth is wide open and the tongue is down. The tongue is positioned towards the middle of the mouth.

The "u" sound in *color* is a short vowel sound. The mouth is relaxed and only partially open. The tongue is positioned towards the middle of the mouth.

By the way, remember the *color, collar,* and *caller* comparison made earlier in this chapter? Well, here's how caller fits into the picture. The "aw" sound in "caller" is a little longer than "color" but a little shorter than "collar." As discussed in "low" vs. "law," the lips move forward slightly and the tongue is positioned toward the back of the mouth to form the "aw" sound. Now back to the "collar" and "color" comparison.

See how well you can differentiate between the following pairs of words:

"AH" Sound	*"U" Sound*
calm	come
stock	stuck
cot	cut
cop	cup
shot	shut
doll	dull
not	nut
fond	fund
rob	rub
hot	hut

PRACTICE WORDS AND SENTENCES

The "AH" Sound

dollar	oxygen	conscious	problem
odd	scholarship	commerce	hospital
property	occupied	golf	options
monopoly	positive	doctor	

The "U" Sound

does	flood	lunch	hundred
month	enough	money	sum
public	dozen	interrupt	deluxe
something	nothing	budget	abrupt
customs	country	subject	

The doctor knew nothing about the scholarship.

Public hospitals have budget problems.

Next month we'll have some more options.

Differentiating Between "Odd" vs. "Add"

What's the difference?

The "a" sound in "*add*" is a short vowel sound. The tongue is positioned towards the front of the mouth and the tongue tip actually touches the lower teeth. The mouth position is not quite as open as the "ah" sound in "*odd*."

If you learned British English you may not always feel comfortable making this short "a" sound. For example, in a word like "last," if your mouth opens too wide, the vowel sound will change to "lah-h-st." On the other hand, there are some American-born speakers who pinch and nasalize the short "a" sound so "last" sounds more like "laaaast." The correct sound is not nasal and not British but somewhere in between the two. Contrast the following words:

Short "A"	*Long "AH"*
rack	rock
hat	hot
packct	pocket
pat	pot
black	block
map	mop
lack	lock
sack	sock
adapt	adopt
racquet	rocket

PRACTICE SENTENCES

I understand you may need to operate.

Nobody has an answer to the problem.

What is the balance on the property?

Saying "Mat" and "Met" Correctly

To many foreigners, "mat" and "met" sound exactly the same, but there is a difference between these two sounds. While both sounds are short, the vowel sound in *mat* is slightly longer than the vowel sound in *met*. Also, in *mat* the mouth position is a little more open and the sound is made slightly farther back in the mouth. The tongue is positioned towards the front of the mouth for both sounds.

Here are some contrasting words to practice:

Short (Lax) "A"	*Short (Lax) "E"*
sad	said
band	bend
had	head

Short (Lax) "A"	*Short (Lax) "E"*
laughed	left
bland	blend
land	lend
gas	guess
man	men
sand	send
tan	ten

PRACTICE SENTENCES

We already sent the packet of materials.

You need to estimate the damage.

The head of this division is inadequate.

Pronouncing "Her" and "Hair" Correctly

What's the difference?

The "ur" sound in *her* is a short vowel sound. The lips push forward slightly and are somewhat rounded.

The "air" sound in *hair* is formed by joining the long "ay" sound (as in letter "a" of the alphabet) with the "r" sound as in "ay-r."

Make sure you make a strong "r" on both sounds. One of my French students had a habit of dropping the "r" sound in "work." Whenever she wanted to say "I went to *work*," it sounded more like "I went to *walk*."

Practice contrasting these words:

"UR"	*"AIR"*
were	wear
blur	blare
stir	stare

spur	spare
fur	fair
curd	cared
purr	pair
hurry	hairy

PRACTICE SENTENCES

Claire was served downstairs.

They're certainly not prepared.

Herb buried himself in his work.

Pronouncing "Firm" and "Farm" Correctly

You wouldn't want to tell a prospective employer that you've worked in a law *farm* when you really meant a law *firm*! But that's just what can happen if you're not careful. Remember, to make the "ur" sound in "firm," keep the mouth only partially open and push the lips slightly forward. To make the "ar" sound in "farm," open the mouth wide and say "ah-h-h" then add the "r" sound as in "ah-r." Here are some contrasting sets to practice:

"UR"	*"AR"*
stir	star
heard	hard
fur	far
burn	barn
hurt	heart
curt	cart
curl	Carl
curve	carve

PRACTICE SENTENCES

Carl threw us a curve at the meeting.

We hear he had a heart attack.

She was the first person to reach the target market.

Finally, watch out for the "u" sound in words like "ed*u*cation" and "man*u*facture." Very often these come out sounding like "*ed-oo*-kay-shun" and "man-*oo*-fak-cher" instead of "*ed-uh*-kay-shun" and "man-*yuh*-fak-cher." Here are a few other words to look at:

Document: Don't say: "dok-*oo*-ment," say: "dok-*yuh*-ment."

Graduate: Don't say: "*grad*-oo-ate," say: "*graj*-oo-ate."

Individual: Don't say: "in-duh-*vid*-oo-uhl," say: "in-duh-*vij*-oo-uhl."

Situation: Don't say: "*sit*-oo-ay-shun," say: "*sich*-oo-ay-shun."

The subtle pronunciation differences between certain groups of sounds is what makes vowels so confusing. Remember, don't let your ears do all the work. Hearing the difference between vowels is only the first step. You must be able to *feel* the difference as well. Once you become more sensitized to how the muscles in the mouth form each sound and where the sound is coming from inside the mouth, you'll really start to get the hang of it. Then, when you're ready, go on and tackle the most troublesome consonants.

PRONOUNCING CONSONANTS CORRECTLY TO SAY WHAT YOU MEAN

It was one of those hot, steamy summer days in New York and my mother, feeling sorry for the workers in her building, offered one of the foreign elevator operators a soda. He enthusiastically accepted. When she asked if he wanted *ice* in it, he looked puzzled for a moment, then laughed and politely said no. It turned out, he thought she had asked if he wanted *eyes* in his soda!

On the first day of school, one of my Asian students at New York University asked to be seated in the front row of the classroom. He explained, "I have very bad *fishin*." He meant to say *vision* but he didn't buzz on the "v" and "zh" sounds.

At a party one of my students once asked for a *chin* and tonic. Of course, what he meant to say was *gin* and tonic but he didn't buzz on the "j" sound.

When non-native speakers of English say "ice" for "eyes" it may reflect the fact that their native language makes no distinction between those two sounds in those particular words. Or their native language may have a rule that changes "s" to "z" in that grouping. It's not that they don't know the voiced/voiceless contrast, because that is present in *all* human languages. But certain English consonant sounds—like "s" and "z"—occur in pairs, one of which is voiced and the other voiceless, and these can cause foreign speakers a variety of different problems.

For any sounds of English that can be hissed, buzzed, or hummed—the way all vowels and the consonants "s, sh, z, zh" can, for example—you will remember that it's easy for you to find out which one you're using. When you put your fingertips on the front of your throat and say "zzzzz" (or a prolonged "zh") the vibration you feel is *voicing*. When you do the same thing and say "sssss" (or a prolonged "sh") you feel no vibration because the sound is *voiceless*. If you're not sure whether you're saying "ice" or "eyes," you can check it this way.

Often, however, you can't use this method, because (1) all English vowels are voiced, and (2) many English consonants can't be pronounced alone. Take the "p" sound; if you try to say it all by itself, you'll find it's impossible. You can only say it with a vowel before or after it, as in "up" or "pie." And when you say those two words with your fingertips on your throat, you feel the vibration caused by the vowel. This means that you can't find out whether people will hear you saying "pie" when you mean "buy" (or vice versa) by trying to feel the vibration.

Paired Sounds

The sounds that can't be said alone and that occur in voiced/voiceless pairs are these:

Voiceless	Voiced	
p	b	(as in "pit" and "bit")
t	d	(as in "tot" and "dot")
k	g	(as in "Kate" and "gate")
ch	j	(as in "chill" and "Jill")

(**Note:** The "ch" sound is really "t" followed by "sh"; the "j" sound is really "d" followed by "zh.")

If your own language doesn't divide these sounds up the same way that English does, these pairs will be a challenge for you. You will need to practice them with a native speaker of English or a tape so that you can learn to keep them straight.

Pronouncing "S" and "Z" Correctly

Most foreigners don't have difficulty forming the "s" and "z" sounds. The problem is knowing when to use which sound. Many times a word is spelled with the letter "s" but pronounced with a buzzing "z" as in the word "music" (méw-zik). There are three rules that will help and are worth discussing briefly.

Rule 1.   The English plural ending never allows two consonants to be pronounced *together* unless they are both voiced or both voiceless, no matter *how* they are spelled.

Rule 2.   English never allows *two* hissing or buzzing sounds to be pronounced together; they have to be separated by a vowel.

Rule 3.   The English plural ending, no matter how it is spelled, will be voiced if it follows a vowel.

These rules will tell you that the "s" of "jumps" will be pronounced "s," because it follows voiceless "p." But the "s" in "bends" will be pronounced "z" because it follows voiced "d." The rules will tell you that the "d" of "jumped" is pronounced "t"—because "t" is voiceless and it follows voiceless "p." (Don't be confused by the fact that "jumped" is *spelled* with a silent vowel between "p" and "d." Pay attention only to the sounds that are pronounced.) The rules will also tell you that the "s" of "peaches" is pronounced "z" because it follows a vowel that is pronounced.

But what do you do when you can't rely on these rules? How do you know whether to use the voiced or voiceless sound? Your best strategy is to go to your dictionary whenever you are unsure about your choice.

Practicing the "S" and "Z" Sounds: "Ice" vs. "Eyes"

What's the difference?

The "s" sound in *ice* is a hissing sound (like a tea kettle) with no vibration. The "z" sound in *eyes* is a buzzing sound (like a bee) made with the vibration of the vocal cords. With your fingertips against the front of your throat, feel the difference between the "s" and "z" sounds as you read aloud each word from left to right:

"S"	"Z"
race	raise
loose	lose
sink	zinc
cease	seize
face	phase
place	plays
loss	laws
price	prize
rice	rise
precedent	president

PRACTICE WORDS AND SENTENCES.   Here is a list of words where letter "s" is pronounced as "z."

because	is	does	proposal
those	physician	deposit	phase
enclose	transition	acquisition	dissolve
dessert	Ms.	news	positive
easy	chosen	has	his
these	was	lose	whose
resolve	choose	reason	confuse
visa	please	observe	wise
resort	busy	museum	compromise
design	clause	thousand	always
resign	resume	result	franchise
designate	poison	cleanse	represent
reserve	residential	residual	feasible
exercise	invisible	advertise	surprise
Tuesday	Wednesday	Thursday	

The *president* set a dangerous *precedent*.

In the *race* against time, I got a *raise*.

Don't lose *face* in the second *phase*.

PRACTICE WORDS AND SENTENCES

"SH" Words

precious	militia	machine	anxious
pressure	issue	conscious	commercial
social	sure	Chicago	
pension	chef		

"ZH" Words

pleasure	measure	usually	division
decision	revision	occasion	leisure
visual	casual	confusion	sabotage
garage	massage	persuasion	treasurer
Asian	prestige		

Here are some sentences contrasting the "*sh*" and "*zh*" sounds:

All the visual aids were sent to Chicago.

The treasurer has a good pension plan.

Buying precious metals is a tough decision.

Pronouncing "CH" and "J" Correctly: "Cheap" vs. "Jeep"

What's the difference?

The "ch" in *cheap* is a voiceless sound. It is a combination of two voiceless sounds "t" and "sh." Say "t—sh." Now join these two sounds together and say "tsh." You should feel an explosion of air, similar to a sneeze "*aa-choo.*"

Practice contrasting these sounds.

"CH"	"J"
choke	joke
etch	edge
rich	ridge
batch	badge
chest	jest
cheer	jeer
chill	Jill
"H"	age
chain	Jane
choice	Joyce

Practice Words and Sentences

"CH" Words

(Be aware of some tricky spellings.)

question	natural	future	century
mutual	congratulate	picture	virtual
situation	fortunate	suggestion	

"J" Words

page	educate	graduate	schedule
individual	register	stage	wage
package	college	manage	
lounge	language	advantage	
mileage	damage	image	

Most of the rich families live on the ridge.

The used jeep was very cheap.

Choking is not a joking matter.

The individual suggested two mutual funds.

There's a question about the schedule.

Fortunately, the soldier has a lot of courage.

Pronouncing "CH" and "SH" Correctly: "Chair" vs. "Share"

Imagine telling an important client that the CEO of your company is also the *Share*man of the Board. Or introducing a key shareholder as a *chair*holder. For foreigners who confuse "ch" and "sh," these are very real traps. Remember, "ch" is a combination of two sounds ("t" and "sh") made with an explosion of air while "sh" is only one sound made with a smooth stream of air. Read each of the following from left to right.

"CH"	*"SH"*
chip	ship
cheat	sheet
chop	shop
cheap	sheep
cheese	she's
catch	cash
ditch	dish
match	mash
watch	wash
which	wish

PRACTICE SENTENCES

Please ship the computer chips.

The winner of the match gets a cash prize.

I wish you would watch more closely.

Pronouncing "Y" and "J" Correctly

What's the difference?

To make the "y" sound in yellow, spread the lips apart and raise the back of the tongue. Then, using the voice, glide into the vowel as in "yeh" for "yellow." To feel the back of the tongue moving up and down on the "y" sound, practice saying the expression "áhee *y*áhee *y*áhee." Remember, the "y" sound is a gliding sound. The "j" sound in "Jell-O" is a much more abrupt sound with no gliding effect; to make it, you have to begin by touching your tongue tip to the bony ridge just behind your upper teeth. Your tongue never does this when you say "y."

One time a Spanish consultant came into a lesson bubbling with enthusiasm. Her husband was a doctor doing his residency and she exclaimed, "I just got the news, my husband will be going to jail!" What she meant to say was "Yale."

Read each word aloud from left to right.

"Y" (Tongue stays down)	"J" (Tongue touches top of mouth in back of teeth)
yet	jet
yolk	joke
year	jeer
mayor	major
yell	gel
you	Jew
use (noun)	juice

PRACTICE SENTENCES

The new *jet* wasn't ready *yet.*

Soon *you'll* have a new *jewel.*

The *mayor* won a *major* victory.

Pronouncing "Y" and "CH" Correctly

If you kicked the habit, you wouldn't want to tell someone "I *choose* to smoke" when you really want to say "I *used* to smoke." But some non-native speakers make this mistake. As is true for "j," you pronounce "ch" by touching your tongue tip to your gums behind your upper teeth.

"CH" (Tongue goes up)	"Y" (Tongue goes down)
chess	yes
choose	use (verb)
cheer	year

PRACTICE SENTENCES

You should always chew your food.

I'll use whichever one I choose.

She'll be a cheerleader next year.

Liquid Sounds

Not all pronunciation problems for foreign speakers are caused by voicing. For example, both English "r" and English "l" are always voiced; but many foreigners have difficulty using them correctly. "R" and "l" may seem to be very different sounds, but they both come from the class of sounds that are known as *liquids*. Many languages have only *one* such sound; others have more liquids than English does. These speakers will often substitute the liquid sound from their own language or follow its rules for liquids instead of the English ones. (Just as English speakers who say "pizza" substitute English "ts" for the Italian double "z.")

The exercises and drills that follow will give you practice with the English "r" and "l" sounds, as well as some other miscellaneous problem sounds and contrasts. When possible, practice them with a native speaker of English or with a tape, to make it easier for you to be sure you're using the right sound.

Pronouncing "R" and "L" Correctly: "Rate" vs. "Late"

To make the "r" sound in *rate*, move the tongue back and let the sides of the tongue touch the sides of the upper teeth. Don't let the tongue tip touch the roof of the mouth until you say the final "t." Make a vibrating sound similar to a growl.

To make the "l" sound in *late* raise the tip of the tongue so that it touches just behind the upper front teeth. Keep the back of the tongue down. Make a vibrating sound as the air escapes over the sides of the tongue.

Making a clear distinction between "r" and "l" is especially difficult for many Asian speakers. If the tongue is not in the right position it's easy for "fried rice" to become "flied lice"!

Read each word aloud from left to right:

"R"	"L"
read	lead
right	light
red	led
wrong	long
crime	climb
praise	plays
fright	flight
store	stall
appear	appeal
corroborate	collaborate

PRACTICE SENTENCES

Make a right at the second light.

The crew didn't have a clue what was wrong.

It doesn't appear that they'll be making an appeal.

Practicing "R" and "L" in the Same Word

Things can really get complicated when "r" and "l" appear in the same word. Take a look at the words that follow:

really	realize	regular	reality
realtor	retailer	railroad	rivalry
several	airmail	clearly	parallel
properly	quarterly	floral	morale
rural	apparel	cultural	liberal

Pronouncing "R" and "W" Correctly: "Run" vs. "Won"

Some non-native speakers substitute "w" for "r." This habit proved to be very frustrating for one of my French students. Every time he would order a glass of red wine at a restaurant the waiter would inevitably deliver white wine instead. What happened was the Frenchman's pronunciation of *red* came out like *wet* and with his heavy accent, "wet wine" sounded more like *white*. To prevent "r" from sounding too much like "w," make sure that you don't push the lips out when trying to form an "r" sound. The tongue should be doing all the work. Practice these contrasting sounds:

"R"	*"W"*
ride	wide
rent	went
rare	wear
rest	west
rye	why
raid	weighed
right	white
rate	wait
ring	wing
roar	war

Practice Sentences

Don't *wait* for a low interest *rate*.

The *rest* of them went out *West*.

Only *one* person can *run* the company.

Pronouncing "V" and "W" Correctly

What's the difference?

To make the "v" sound in "vest," touch your upper front teeth to your lower lip and make a buzzing sound. (If you don't buzz, "v" will sound like "f." For example, "view," without the vibration sounds like "few.")

To make the "w" sound in *west*, round your lips slightly and make a voiced gliding sound. Don't let your bottom lip touch the teeth.

Concentrate on your lips and teeth as you read each word aloud from left to right.

"V" (Teeth touch lip)	*"W" (Teeth and lips don't touch)*
vine	wine
verse	worse
veal	we'll
veer	we're
vault	Walt
visor	wiser
vain	Wayne
vet	wet
vow	wow
vent	went

PRACTICE WORDS AND SENTENCES

vague	void	valid	vacant
voucher	verify	veto	virtual
volume	avoid	advise	convey
invest	divide	convince	November
involve			

we	watch	week	want
won't	world	work	win
Wednesday	warning	always	women
away	someone	sandwich	awkward
waste	waiting		

Make reservations a week in advance.

The Vice President wanted to vote.

I wasn't aware of the investment's value.

Pronouncing "QU" Correctly

Make sure that "question" sounds like "kwés-chun" and not "kvés-chun." Remember that a "qu" spelling really translates into a "kw" sound. So think "kw" whenever you see words like "quality," "quantity," "equal," and so on.

Pronouncing "B" and "V" Correctly: "Boat" vs. "Vote"

What's the difference?

"B" is made with the lips only while "v" is made with the lower lip and upper teeth. Many Asian and Spanish speakers have a hard time differentiating between these two sounds.

"B"	"V"
berry	very
bent	vent
beer	veer
best	vest
base	vase
bolt	volt
bail	veil
marble	marvel
curb	curve

PRACTICE SENTENCES

We think the vent may be bent.

I found the best place to invest.

We all marveled at the beautiful marble statue.

Pronouncing the "N" and "NG" Correctly: "Sin" vs. "Sing"

What's the difference?

In terms of how the tongue is used, the "n" and "ng" sounds are polar opposites. To make the "n," touch the *tip of the tongue* behind the upper front teeth. Let the air escape through the nose.

To make the "ng," raise the *back of the tongue* against the soft palate (the soft area toward the back of the roof of the mouth). Keep the tip of the tongue down behind the lower front teeth. Let the air escape through the nose. Many native Spanish speakers have a particularly tough time distinguishing the "n" and "ng" sounds. Think about your tongue placement as you contrast these words.

"N"	*"NG"*
win	wing
sun	sung
ban	bang
ton	tongue
lawn	long
gone	gong
thin	thing
ran	rang
clan	clang
stun	stung

As you make the "ng," sound be sure that you leave the back of the tongue up against the soft palate until the sound has ended. If you release the tongue too soon, you may get a hard "g" or "k" sound as in "thing-ga" or "thing-k" instead of "thing."

PRACTICE WORDS AND SENTENCES

anxiety	young	hang	along
lung	among	strong	wrong

He is learning the language.

Come along with us to England.

Sandy is looking at it from a different angle.

Pronouncing the "TH" Sounds Correctly

There is one final sound without which no accent reduction program would be complete. It is perhaps the most difficult and confusing sound in all of the English language. I'm talking about the "th" sound in "*th*in" and "*th*is." Depending on where you're from, you may substitute one of several sounds when trying to pronounce "th." For example, "thin" may come out sounding like "tin," "sin," or even "fin"; "this" may come out "zis." For more information on how to tackle this troublesome sound, see Chapter Two.

USING YOUR TONGUE CORRECTLY TO IMPROVE YOUR ENGLISH

As you continue to work on your pronunciation, remember the goal is not to eliminate your accent, but simply to speak clearly and make yourself easily understood. You can make a simple change in your English pronunciation that will improve it dramatically. The English sounds written "t, d, n, l, ch, j" all require the tip of the tongue to touch the bony ridge just in back of the upper teeth, called the *alveolar ridge*. They are alveolar sounds in English. In many other languages, however, these sounds are *dental* instead of alveolar, and are pronounced by putting the tip of the tongue against the back of the upper teeth themselves.

Say the following words, paying close attention to *where* your tongue touches the top of your mouth for the first sound in the word:

tea	dog
nice	look
chin	jug

If your tongue touched the back of your teeth as you did this, you didn't sound English. Say the words again and deliberately touch your tongue to the ridge *behind* your upper teeth as you say "t, d, n, l, ch, j." Do the same thing whenever you pronounce these sounds, no matter where they are in the word. It will improve your English greatly to make this one change, which—unlike many other changes—is under your conscious control. (Speakers of English have exactly the same problem in reverse when they learn foreign languages; they have a foreign accent because they pronounce these sounds as alveolars instead of dentals. If you have an English-speaking friend who is trying to learn French or Spanish, pass this hint along.)

Say It Out Loud!

Here are six brief quotations that you can read aloud (and/or memorize to say aloud without reading) as a way to practice what you've learned about how to diminish your accent. Aim for "standard" pronunciation of American English.

In the first quote, pay particular attention to the pronunciation of "s" and "z."

In the 1970s . . . Roger Schank outlined a theory of artificial intelligence known today as case-based reasoning. Schank . . . explains what this is: "Case-based reasoning organizes information on the basis of concepts, not exact answers."

DAVID C. CHURBUCK,
"Learning by Example," *Forbes* Magazine, June 8, 1992, p. 130.

It's part of my challenge to make sure complacency doesn't set in, to maintain a sense of urgency as we pursue excellence.

HANS BECHERER,
quoted in Reed Ableson et al., "Corporate Leaders: Is There a Doctor in the House?," *Forbes* Magazine, May 28, 1990, p. 219.

In choosing people for top positions, you have to try to make sure they have a clear sense of what is right and wrong, a willingness to be truthful, the courage to say what they think and to do what they think is right . . .

W. MICHAEL BLUMENTHAL,
quoted in Jerry Flint, "Master of the Game," *Forbes* Magazine, May 28, 1990, p. 200.

In the following quotation, pay particular attention to the "w" sound:

The key question every successful manager has to ask is not "Why did we win?" but "Why did the other guys lose?" This may seem a bit like rain on your victory parade, but it's the only way to be sure you'll get to march in another one.

BILL WALSH,
"Succeeding Despite Success," *Forbes ASAP,* September 13, 1993, p. 17.

Here's a good quotation to help you practice the "l" sound:

When an overseas visitor arrives late at night at the Lego hotel, a Lego executive calls to make sure he is comfortable. The next day the visitor's national flag is snapping from a corporate flagpole. . . . Only the most churlish customer could resist such stroking.

RICHARD C. MORAIS,
"Babes in Toyland?," *Forbes* Magazine, January 3, 1994, p. 71.

The biggest mistake a coach or an executive can make after beating the competition is to assume that the best team or company won. . . . As often as not, losers beat themselves and hand the victory to their opponents.

BILL WALSH,
"Succeeding Despite Success," *Forbes ASAP,* September 13, 1993, p. 17.

Part 2

Building Your
Vocal Advantage

6

Adding Power and Authority to Your Voice to Achieve Your Goals

HOW VOCAL GENDER CONFUSION CAN SHAKE YOUR CONFIDENCE

Tracy Cheswick knew he wasn't going to be able to close this sale; he could tell from the voice on the other end of the phone line. But that was okay; sometimes it took a lot more than just one sales call to land a new account. The groundwork he was laying today would serve him well when he came back to this potential customer to try again, and he intended to give her his most effective sales pitch each and every time, until she said yes.

"You know you can count on us for top quality," he said, summing up. "You know your order will be shipped the same day you call it in. You know our service contract is the best in the business. And we are prepared to custom tailor the product to your specific needs—something no other firm in our field can offer you. Just tell me how many units to put you down for!"

There was a short silence, and Tracy was just getting ready to break in with a few more points. And then it happened. . . .

"I'm genuinely sorry, Miss Cheswick," said the voice. "You're very persuasive, but we're happy with our current supplier and we aren't interested in making any changes."

Tracy was so stunned that he completely lost his composure. "Okay!" he said hastily. "Thanks for your time!" and he hung up. It wasn't the way he ordinarily concluded an important sales call like this one, but he knew that if he stayed on the line he'd only make a fool of himself. He was used to having people turn him down; after all, he was selling an expensive product for a relatively new company in a very competitive field. He could handle that. But having a prospect mistake him for a woman? He wasn't at all sure he could handle *that!*

Not because there weren't plenty of women at the very top of his profession. Sure there were, and some of them had higher sales totals than his own. But he was a man. . . . If someone listening to him could assume that his voice was a woman's voice, there had to be something terribly *wrong* with it!

"*My voice is my livelihood,*" he thought; he was badly shaken. "I'd better get cracking and do something about this problem, before I find myself working the counter at a McDonalds!"

HOW A BREATHY, "LITTLE GIRL" VOICE CAN HOLD YOU BACK

Jeanne Clark frowned impatiently at the ringing phone; she was ready to leave for work, and she was already late. For an instant she thought about just letting it ring, and then she shook her head—it might be something important.

"Hello?" she said. "Yes?"

"Is this the Clark residence?"

"Yes, it is," she said sharply. "What do you want?"

The caller cleared his throat, and Jeanne braced herself—if this was one of those aluminum siding salesmen she was going to just hang up on him.

And then it happened. . . .

"Could I talk to your mommy, please?" the voice asked. "Would you ask Mommy to come to the phone, honey?"

Jeanne *did* hang up, without saying another word. *He thought I was a little girl!* she thought, her heart sinking. No *wonder* I'm having such a hard time dealing with customers!

Learning Why We Sound the Way We Do

Embarrassing situations like these are more common than most people think. Grown women with little girl voices, middle-aged men with weak and wimpy voices, the squeaky, the hoarse, the wobbly, and the whisperers account for a surprisingly large sector of the business population. If your voice is more of a liability than an asset, because it falls into one of these groups, then it is time for a change.

While certain physiological factors play a role in how we sound, psychological and social forces are primarily responsible for the sound of the voice. Here are some examples:

- The young woman who through social conditioning is taught to be reserved and "lady-like" may acquire a soft and breathy voice.

- The man who is not pleased with his own sound may develop an affected speech pattern to cover up his vocal inferiority complex.

- The woman who finds it difficult to adjust to aging may acquire a "little girl" sound in an effort to preserve her youth.

- The child who is constantly told "Shh! You'll wake the baby!" may acquire a hushed and breathy tone which can last throughout his adult life.

- The person who comes from a large family may develop a shrill, high-pitched voice in order to be heard above the rest of the noise at the dinner table.

One's personal likes and dislikes also come into play. For example, the fear of sounding too loud, too harsh, too manly, or too effeminate can cause a person to jump to the other extreme. And of course people tend to sound like their parents and siblings; an ineffective voice is often handed down like the family china. The list can go on and on.

While understanding why you sound the way you do may be a good first step, it's not enough to correct the situation. You need a systematic program to strengthen and improve your voice.

Exercising Your Way to a Stronger Voice

One of the most common questions I get asked is, "Can you actually change the sound of a person's voice?" The answer is yes. Just as physical exercise can make your body stronger and healthier, there are exercises that can strengthen your voice. The host of a national TV shopping network was running into trouble. Her voice sounded raspy and would frequently get hoarse toward the end of her show. I received a call from the head of programming at the network who wanted to know what could be done to strengthen her voice. When I prescribed a regimen of daily voice exercises, the executive protested, saying, "But she's on the air 3 hours a day, 5 days a week! Why isn't her voice getting stronger now?" The simple fact is that you can't build a strong and effective voice just by speaking. Ordinary speech doesn't give the voice enough of a workout. To build your voice you need exercises that stretch and sustain sound. Think of them as the "calisthenics" of voice training. They add power and authority to the voice and make it sound deeper, richer, and more resonant. Famous actors use these same techniques to develop their speaking voices for the stage and screen.

Before you begin, we need to cover three important topics: *breathing*, *vocal support*, and *posture*.

HOW TO BREATHE CORRECTLY

Breathe *normally*. Good breathing doesn't require any physical preparation; it should be automatic. Leave the shoulder-raising, tummy tucking, and chest popping to the army. Your goal is to get the most sound with the least effort.

Avoid taking a deep breath before you speak, because sucking in too much air wastes energy and can make you tense. It's not the amount of air that counts; it's how you *use* it. Think of a laughing spell. Free laughter has a great carrying power and can be sustained for a long time without conscious intake of air.

Many speakers can benefit from learning to use their breath more economically. If you use too much breath at the beginning of a phrase, you may not have enough left to finish your phrase. This can cause the ends of your phrases to become inaudible or trail off. Learning proper breath control will help you make the most of your breath supply, so that you can fully sustain your sound.

Think of a rubber duck bath toy. When you squeeze it, air is forced out. When the pressure is released, the toy again sucks up the air it needs to regain its shape. The human breathing pattern is very similar: All you need to do is replace the air you breathe out. Breathe out; then replace. A natural intake of air will help you achieve a more effortless production of sound.

Very often too much attention is focused on breathing because the breath is the easiest part of the vocal process to isolate. Many people think that learning how to breathe correctly is the answer to all their vocal problems. This usually isn't the case. A master breather doesn't make a master speaker. Keep in mind that the production of sound in speech involves the coordination of several functions that work together simultaneously: the *breath*, the *vocal cords*, and the *resonance cavities*. Sound is produced by the action of the breath on the vocal cords, which is then resonated in the head and chest. A good voice requires a working balance of all three functions. It's the *coordination* that counts. The best way to judge if everything is working well is by analyzing the final product, the sound. If the sound is full and the production effortless, that means you're breathing correctly.

DEFINING YOUR VOCAL SUPPORT

Vocal support is an inner muscular action that helps to support the voice. The support muscles enable you to produce an even, vibrant flow of sound and sustain long sequences with ease. Think of vocal support as the foundation of your voice. With proper support, your voice can project effortlessly without strain or fatigue. Using your support muscles properly can help a wobbly voice become firmer and steadier.

To feel your support muscles working, try a simple experiment. Do a belly laugh. Free spontaneous laughter has an "innerspring" action that's capable of producing tremendous power and energy. In fact, the midsection of the body may be thought of as the energy center of your voice. When you speak, you're not going to feel the same innerspring action as you do when you laugh; vocal support in speech is much more subtle. However, if you pay close attention when using your full voice, you might be able to sense some muscular action in the midsection of your body. This sensation means your support muscles are working. Feeling a connection with this center as you speak will help you to sustain a full sound.

Good support requires a balance of *stability* and *flexibility*. Think of how a mattress supports your body. If a mattress is too firm, your body can't relax. However, if a mattress is too soft, your body begins to sag. Vocal support is very similar. Tensing the inner muscles too much can lead to tightening. On the other hand, if the muscles are too loose, your voice may lose its sustaining power. Many speakers make the mistake of pushing from the throat instead of letting the support muscles do the work. All the throat needs to do is stay open and relaxed. Like breathing, vocal support requires no conscious manipulation of muscles. Good support should come naturally, as part of the act of making sound. (Exercises to practice vocal support can be found later in this chapter.)

HOW POSTURE PLAYS AN IMPORTANT ROLE

Good posture allows sound to travel freely and can help you to project the voice. It enables you to produce a full, vibrant sound. However, good posture doesn't mean that you have to stand at attention. Raising your shoulders, sticking out your chest, and sucking in your stomach is overdoing it and can actually make you tense. Here are a few simple rules to follow:

- Stand up straight but not rigid.
- Position your feet carefully, making sure your body is well balanced.
- Relax your shoulders.
- Avoid hunching or slouching. Bad posture prevents the breath from flowing evenly and can constrict your sound.

These same rules apply when speaking from a seated position; people often get a little too comfortable when they're sitting in a chair. This is especially true when talking on the telephone. Because you're heard and not seen, it's easy to become too relaxed and get careless. When this happens, you can lose vocal support and end up speaking from your throat. This puts extra strain on your throat muscles and can cause your voice to tire prematurely. So, if you spend long hours on the phone, be conscious of your posture. Remember that a well-supported voice means fewer problems.

Finally, make an extra effort to avoid drooping, slumping, or sagging when you're tired. Using good posture can give your voice the energy and vitality it needs.

How the 12-Minute Vocal Workout Will Help You Build Your Voice

The 12-Minute Vocal Workout includes *breathing exercises*, *vocalizing techniques*, and *practice words and sentences*. First, you'll build the voice with stretching and sustaining exercises. Then you'll learn how to work back, step by step, and apply the power you're gaining to your speech. In the process, you're going to explore the natural qualities in your voice and build on its strengths.

Start by reading through this chapter to familiarize yourself with the exercises. At first glance, they may seem a little overwhelming, but keep in mind that you're really only looking at about a 12-minute daily workout. As with any exercise program, once you get the hang of the routine, you'll be able to breeze through it. You'll find the exercises simple, easy to learn, and fun too. In fact, after a few run-throughs you'll probably have the whole routine memorized. You can practice in the shower, while getting dressed, driving in your car, or even walking. Be imaginative. One busy executive found time to practice in the elevator when no one else was around, on his way up to his 46th-floor office! On those really hectic days when you can't find a 12-minute block of time, don't give up; do several miniworkouts throughout the day. Remember, for best results, you need to exercise on a regular basis. That's what builds the strength and endurance you want.

DESCRIBING THE VOCAL WORKOUT

First, here's a short outline to give you a breakdown of what the workout consists of.

1. Breathing/Relaxation Exercise . . . . 1 minute

2. Sustained Humming Exercise . . . . 3 minutes

3. Extended Vowel Exercise
   ("m*ah*"/Double "m*ah*", etc.) . . . . 3 minutes

4. Singing Words ("IOWA," etc.) . . . . 3 minutes

5. Sustained Speaking Exercises
   (Practice Words and Sentences). . . . . 2 minutes

Keep in mind that some of these exercises may not sound very pretty. If you don't want anyone else to hear you practice (neighbors, family members, and so forth), here's a good technique to muffle your sound. Hold a pillow about an inch away from your mouth as you practice. The pillow will absorb about 90% of your sound. No one will hear the other 10%. If you use a pillow as a mute, you won't have to hold back when you practice. The main point is, to get the full benefits of the workout you have to use your full voice. Just think, now when you stay at a hotel, there's no excuse not to practice!

As you go through the workout you'll notice that certain sections go well beyond the timings given in this outline. Don't attempt to do all the exercises in each section in a single workout. An assortment of exercises is provided so that you can enjoy some variety in your daily workout. For example, in section 4 ("Singing Words"), on a given day you may select the "IOWA" exercise. The next time you practice you may choose "LULLABY," and so on. Remember, you're only looking at about a 12-minute daily workout.

Now, here's how the exercises work:

1. BREATHING/RELAXATION EXERCISES FOR BETTER BREATH CONTROL (1 MINUTE)

The following exercises will relax the mouth, throat, and jaw and help you achieve better breath control.

Using the breath only (like a whisper), slowly exhale on

"PAH-H-H-H-H-H-H-H-H."

Aim for a long, even-flowing stream of air.

- Don't take in a deep breath before you begin—just breathe normally.
- Let the jaw drop down and open your mouth wide. (Think of the mouth position you use when the doctor examines your throat.)
- Keep the mouth, throat, and jaw relaxed.
- Allow the air to flow out evenly and stop just before you run out of breath. This should feel like a lazy yawn.

Repeat:

"PAH-H-H-H-H-H-H-H-H."

Following the same instructions as above, do a series of four sustained breathing exercises. Pause after each breath to allow your body to naturally replace the air you spend.

"PAH-H-H-H-H-H-H-H-H." (pause)

Now slowly exhale on "Tah."

"TAH-H-H-H-H-H-H-H-H." (pause)

Now exhale on "Kah."

"KAH-H-H-H-H-H-H-H-H." (pause)

Finally, exhale on "Mah."

"MAH-H-H-H-H-H-H-H-H." (pause)

If possible, repeat this series several times throughout the day at about 1-minute intervals.

These easy breathing exercises are also a good stress reducer. The next time you have to give a speech or presentation try a few long, sustained breaths before you begin. This really has a way of calming those last-minute jitters! There's one more benefit: because breathing is silent, these exercises can be done just about anywhere.

2. USING SUSTAINED HUMMING EXERCISES TO FEEL THE POWER AND RESONANCE IN YOUR VOICE

Humming is the quickest and easiest way to feel the power and resonance in your voice. It's an exercise that you're probably familiar with, since many people hum tunes around the house, in the shower, or with the radio.

- With lips together, make a long humming sound.

    "mmmmmmmmmmmmmmmmmmmm"

- Breathe normally.
- Let the air flow out evenly and stop the sound just before you run out of breath.

As you hum, be aware of any buzzing, vibrating, or tickling sensations in the lips, nose, throat, and chest. These are all signs of resonance. The more places you can feel these vibrations, the fuller and richer your sound will be. Think of the following images to help you buzz along: a bumblebee, vacuum cleaner, buzz saw, outboard motor, electric shaver, or a purring cat. Repeat the long humming sound:

    "mmmmmmmmmmmmmmmmmmmm"

Practicing the Humming Scale for Resonance (3 minutes)

Do a series of sustained humming sounds going up and down your voice range. Imagine humming up and down a scale ("do" "re" "mi" "fa" "sol," and so on). Practice only what feels comfortable. If a note feels too high or too low, leave it out for now. If you're having trouble following a scale, don't worry. Just try to hum a variety of sounds, since the sequence doesn't really matter. Don't let the pitch distract you. Keep in mind, this is not a pitch exercise, but a *voice building* exercise. If you concentrate on feeling resonance, you'll get good results. Start on a low pitch. Note by note, work your way up to the top. Then, note by note, come down again. Go up and down the following scale pattern starting with 1 and ending with 9. Pause for a breath after each humming sound. (See the diagram below.)

Concentrate on feeling resonance. You want to find the part of your range where you feel the most vibrations, because this is where your voice is strongest. For example, if you feel more vibrations in the lower part of your range, this indicates that your natural speaking voice is low. As you work your way down in pitch, you may start to feel more vibrations in the chest. This is known as *chest resonance*. Speaking with chest resonance adds depth and authority to your voice. Repeat the humming scale.

5. mmmmmmmmmm

(pause)

4. mmmmmmmmmm   mmmmmmmmmm 6.

(pause)   *(pause)*

3. mmmmmmmmmm   mmmmmmmmmm 7.

(pause)   *(pause)*

2. mmmmmmmmmm   mmmmmmmmmm 8.

(pause)   *(pause)*

1. mmmmmmmmmm   mmmmmmmmmm 9.

In addition to building resonance, humming is also a great way to warm up the voice. The next time you have some important speaking to do, try to make a few humming sounds before you begin. When you can't find a place for lengthy practice, here's a quick exercise you can do just about anywhere.

Using the Quick Sliding Hum for Chest Resonance

In one breath, make a humming sound on a high pitch and then quickly slide down to a low pitch. Let the voice drop into the chest area. This helps the rich chest resonance kick in when you start to speak. The sliding hum is short and fast, and should only last a few seconds. Do a couple of quick sliding humming sounds. Pause for a breath after each sliding hum.

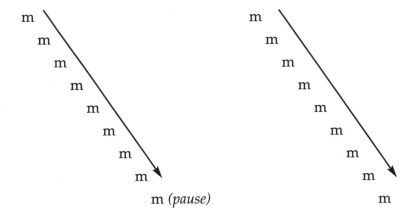

A female financial executive was known throughout her department for her distinctive squeaky, Betty Boop-like voice. (She even got offers from casting agents to do radio commercials!) One day, as an experiment, she decided to do a quick sliding hum each time before picking up the phone. Her voice dropped down so low that when several of her associates called that day they didn't even know she was the one speaking.

Do the quick sliding hum throughout the course of your day. It's a great way to rev up your voice. And by activating the lower chest resonance, it assures you of a strong start.

3. PRACTICING EXTENDED VOWEL EXERCISES FOR RESONANCE AND POWER

Think of a vowel as a "storage unit" for sound. Practicing vowel sounds brings out the resonance in the voice and gives it more carrying power. If you're like most people, you probably don't open your mouth and throat wide enough when you speak. This can cut your sound in half. Working on sustained vowel exercises strengthens your voice and helps to free your sound of any constriction. In fact, studies have shown that many people with stuttering problems don't stutter when they sing. Learning to apply this freedom to one's speech can often be an effective treatment for stutterers.

Carrying Resonance into the Vowel Sound with the Sustained "mAH" Exercise

Begin with a humming sound. After a second or two, without stopping the sound, open the mouth wide and make an "ah" sound. (This is the same sound you would make when the doctor examines your throat.) Let the hum lead directly into the vowel sound.

"mmmmmmmmmmmmmmAH-H-H-H-H-H-H-H-H-H"

The aim is to take the resonance from the humming sound and carry it over into the vowel sound. Remember to breathe normally. Repeat:

"mmmmmmmmmmmmmmAH-H-H-H-H-H-H-H-H-H"

Using the "mAH" Scale to Build Power (2 minutes)

Do a series of long, sustained "mAH" sounds going up and down your range. Start on a low pitch and work your way up and down the scale, note by note. Only practice what feels comfortable. Pause for a breath after each long "mAH" sound.

5. mmmAH-H-H-H

4. mmmAH-H-H-H   mmmAH-H-H-H 6.

3. mmmAH-H-H-H   mmmAH-H-H-H 7.

2. mmmAH-H-H-H   mmmAH-H-H-H 8.

1. mmmAH-H-H-H   mmmAH-H-H-H 9.

Concentrate on feeling resonance in your head and chest. Keep in mind that because the lips are apart on the open "ah" sound, you may not feel the same buzzing or tickling sensations as you did in the humming sound. However, you may feel resonance in other places, including the throat and chest. If you're having trouble feeling any vibrations at first, place your hand over your chest as you practice. This should help.

- Try to keep track of where you feel the most vibrations—the upper, middle, or lower part of your range.
- Imagine you're calling out to someone, but don't shout. This can strain the voice.
- Strive for a clear and ringing sound. This gives the voice its carrying power.

By the way, if you experience a slight wavering in your voice, don't worry. This doesn't mean you have a wobble. This pulsating effect is known as *vibrato*. You're in good company; all well-trained singers have vibrato, which enhances their sound. So if your voice wants to pulsate, let it go. Don't try to control it. And don't be concerned that vibrato will affect your speaking voice. Vibrato will not enter into your speech because speech sounds are less sustained than singing sounds.

Practicing the Double "mAH" Exercise
for Breath Control and Sustained Power

To improve breath control and build sustained power, practice *two* long "mAH" sounds in each breath. Your goal is to make two full, resonant tones without stopping the sound:

"MmmmAH-H-HmmmmAH-H-H-H-H."

Make sure you have enough breath left over for the second "mAH" sound. Don't spend all your breath at once. Save your breath! Repeat:

"mmmmAH-H-HmmmmAH-H-H-H-H."

How the Double "mAH" Scale Makes Your Muscles Work (2 minutes)

Start on a low pitch. Note by note, work your way up to the top. Then, note by note, come down again. Pause for a breath after each long double "mAH" sound. (As before, don't worry if your scale isn't perfect.)

- *Be aware of your support muscles working.* See if you can sense an inner muscle action as you vocalize. You may experience a certain degree of tension or pushing of the muscles around the midsection of the body. Remember, don't consciously tense these muscles. Let this happen on its own.

- *Listen for the ring and echo in your voice.* This reverberation is a sign of resonance. The more ring, the better.

5. mmAH-HmmAH-H

4. mmAH-HmmAH-H   mmAH-HmmAH-H 6.

3. mmAH-HmmAH-H   mmAH-HmmAH-H 7.

2. mmAH-HmmAH-H   mmAH-HmmAH-H 8.

1. mmAH-HmmAH-H   mmAH-HmmAH-H 9.

How the Double "mAH" Drop Helps Lower the Pitch of Your Voice (1/2–1 minute)

This is a good technique to help lower the pitch of your voice. Make a double "mAH" sound again, but this time change pitch on the second "mAH" sound. Start your first "mAH" on a mid-range note, then in the same breath, drop down to a low note on your second "mAH" sound. It should look something like this:

mmmmAH-H-H-H-H ⌐

                ↓

         mmmmAH-H-H-H-H

Make sure you start high enough so you have enough room left to drop down in pitch. (If you're still unable to reach the lower note, you may be dropping down too far.) Try the Double "mAH" Drop on a variety of notes until the lower note gets too low. Remember, only practice what feels comfortable. You can always begin the sequence again on a higher note and work your way down. If your voice is stronger in the middle to upper range and weaker in the lower range, this "dropping down" technique will help carry the strength and resonance farther down to where you want it.

Of course, there are those rare cases where a person may want just the opposite. I once trained a female psychiatrist who had such low pitch that over the phone prospective patients thought that she was a man. This led to some very embarrassing face-to-face encounters. Here was a woman who actually needed a *higher* voice! This was a very unusual situation; as a rule, women with deep voices should welcome their lower tones. After all, a deep voice has a commanding presence. Just think of Kathleen Turner and Candice Bergen.

4. SINGING WORDS TO INCREASE YOUR RESONANCE

Now that you've practiced humming and "mAH" sounds, it's time to work on some real words. Each word contains a variety of vowel sounds. Practicing sustained vowel combinations will strengthen the vowel sounds in your speech. This will help make your speaking voice more resonant. The aim is to feel vibration on every vowel sound; try to make all the vowels resonate.

Don't attempt to do all the words listed here in one practice session. Instead, alternate words each time you practice.

Using the IOWA Exercise

In one breath, sustain the three vowel sounds, I, OH, and AH. Don't stop the sound between each vowel. Instead connect each vowel sound to the other. It should sound like you're singing the word "IOWA."

- Keep the sound full from start to finish.
- Open the mouth wide on each vowel.
- Relax the mouth, throat, and jaw.
- Breathe normally.

Repeat: "I----------------yO----------------WA----------------"

Adding a little "y" sound before the "O" vowel helps keep the sound continuous from "I" to "O."

Singing the IOWA Scale (2–3 minutes)

Start on a low pitch. Work your way up and down the scale, note by note, practicing only what feels comfortable.

Pause for a breath after each long I-yO-WA sound.

```
                         5. I------yO------WA-----

          4. I------yO------WA-----        I------yO------WA----- 6.

     3. I------yO------WA-----                  I------yO------WA----- 7.

  2. I------yO------WA-----                         I------yO------WA----- 8.

1. I------yO------WA-----                                I------yO------WA----- 9.
```

Practicing the IOWA Drop (1/2–1 minute)

Try the same technique you used with the "Double mAH Drop" on "IOWA." Start the first vowel "I" on a middle note, then, in the same breath, drop down to a low note on the last two vowels "O" and "WA." It should look something like this:

Try the IOWA Drop on a variety of notes until the lower note gets too low.

Using the LULLABY Exercise

In one breath, sustain these three syllables:

LUH---------------LUH---------------BY---------------

Don't let the consonants crowd the vowels. Remember, most consonants *articulate* sound; vowels *project* sound. To allow the voice to resonate freely, you need to keep your vowels full and open. Also, when practicing sustained vowel exercises, don't be concerned about precise pronunciation. To keep your vowels open and free, it's okay to cheat a little. You can even change "LUH-LUH-BY" to "LAH-LAH-BY" to help you feel maximum resonance. Keep in mind that even professional opera singers sometimes modify pronunciation to produce the best sound.

Singing the LULLABY Scale (2–3 minutes)

Start on a low pitch and work your way up and down the scale note by note.

5. LUH-LUH-BY

4. LUH-LUH-BY   LUH-LUH-BY 6.

3. LUH-LUH-BY   LUH-LUH-BY 7.

2. LUH-LUH-BY   LUH-LUH-BY 8.

1. LUH-LUH-BY   LUH-LUH-BY 9.

Practicing the LULLABY Drop (1/2-1 minute)

Practice the "Lullaby Drop" on a variety of notes until the lower note gets too low.

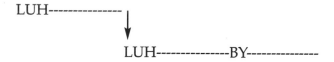

LUH-------------

LUH-------------BY-------------

Using the DYNAMO Exercise

In one breath, sustain these three syllables:

DY---------------NA---------------MO--------------

Remember to open the mouth wide on each vowel sound. Relax the mouth, throat, and jaw and breathe normally.

Singing the DYNAMO Scale (2-3 minutes)

Start on a low pitch and work your way up and down the scale note by note.

```
                    5. DY-NA-MO

        4. DY-NA-MO                  DY-NA-MO 6.

      3. DY-NA-MO                      DY-NA-MO 7.

    2. DY-NA-MO                          DY-NA-MO 8.

  1. DY-NA-MO                              DY-NA-MO 9.
```

Practicing the DYNAMO Drop (1/2-1 minute)

Practice the "DYNAMO Drop" on a variety of notes until the lower note gets too low.

Using the DIALOG Exercise

In one breath, sustain these three syllables:

DI---------------yA---------------LO---------------G

Adding a little "y" sound before the "A" vowel helps keep the sound continuous from "DI" to "A." Don't worry about the final "g" sound on "DIALOG"; for now, keep the focus on the vowels.

Singing the DIALOG Scale (2–3 minutes)

Start on a low pitch and work your way up and down the scale note by note.

<pre>
                        5. DI-yA-LOG

          4. DI-yA-LOG   DI-yA-LOG 6.

         3. DI-yA-LOG   DI-yA-LOG 7.

        2. DI-yA-LOG   DI-yA-LOG 8.

      1. DI-yA-LOG   DI-yA-LOG 9.
</pre>

Practicing the DIALOG Drop (1/2 minute–1 minute)

Practice the "Dialog Drop" on a variety of notes until the lower note gets too low.

Using the LIONEL Exercise

In one breath, sustain these three syllables:

LI--------------yO--------------NE-------------L

Adding a little "y" sound before "O" helps keep the sound continuous from "LI" to "O." Add the final "L" at the very last second so it doesn't interfere with the vowel sound that precedes it.

Singing the LIONEL Scale (2-3 minutes)

Start with a low pitch and work your way up and down the scale note by note.

```
                              5. LI-yO-NEL
         4. LI-yO-NEL                      LI-yO-NEL 6.
         3. LI-yO-NEL                      LI-yO-NEL 7.
      2. LI-yO-NEL                            LI-yO-NEL 8.
   1. LI-yO-NEL                                  LI-yO-NEL 9.
```

Practicing the LIONEL Drop

Practice the "LIONEL Drop" on a variety of notes until the lower note gets too low.

LI--------------
                ↓
        yO--------------NE--------------L

Using the LAYAWAY Exercise

In one breath, sustain these three syllables:

LAY--------------yA--------------WAY--------------

Adding a little "y" sound before the "A" vowel helps keep the sound continuous from "LAY" to "A."

Singing the LAYAWAY Scale (2-3 minutes)

Start on a low pitch and work your way up and down the scale note by note. Pause for a breath after each LAY-yA-WAY sound.

5. LAY-yA-WAY

4. LAY-yA-WAY   LAY-yA-WAY 6.

3. LAY-yA-WAY   LAY-yA-WAY 7.

2. LAY-yA-WAY   LAY-yA-WAY 8.

1. LAY-yA-WAY   LAY-yA-WAY 9.

Practicing the LAYAWAY Drop (1/2-1 minute)

Practice the "LAYAWAY Drop" on a variety of notes until the lower note gets too low.

For additional words to work on, choose some of the practice words in the next section. Select those words that are the easiest for you to "sing." For example, a word such as "Amazon" may flow better than a word like "absolutely."

5. USING SUSTAINED SPEAKING EXERCISES TO HELP BUILD RESONANCE

Now it's time to take the power you're gaining in the singing techniques and apply it to the spoken word. The following words and phrases are designed to strengthen the vowels in your speech. This will help build resonance in your speaking voice. Keep in mind that this is an exaggerated exercise. You still need to stretch and sustain sounds. The difference is that you're now speaking words, not singing words.

PRACTICE WORDS AND SENTENCES (2 MINUTES).   There are far too many practice words and sentences here to do in a single workout. You only need to do a couple minutes of these words and sentences every day. Each time you practice, simply pick up where you left off until you have completed all the practice words. Then start over again.

Practice each word separately, saying one word in each breath. Using your full voice, slightly elongate the words and emphasize the vowel sounds. For example, if the practice word is "agenda," it should look something like this:

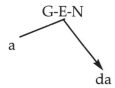

- Use a lot of inflection. Let your voice go where it wants to. (Where it ends up may surprise you!) Allowing the voice to travel freely will help you find your *natural* speaking voice.

- Concentrate on feeling resonance vibrations in the head and chest.

- Open wide and relax the mouth, throat, and jaw.

- Breathe normally.

Read the following words aloud from left to right. Repeat each word and sentence several times, trying out different inflection patterns.

abode	agenda	align	annoy
Alabama	alibi	alien	alone
Amanda	amazing	Amazon	Amelia
ammonia	amnesia	analogy	anatomy
anemia	Angela	Anita	anonymous
apology	audio	avail	avenue
avocado	avow	azalea	Apollo

What's on the agenda?

Amelia has no alibi.

Angela is on the avenue.

baby	Babylonian	balcony	ballet
balloon	balmy	bamboo	banana
banjo	bay	beamy	beautify
because	bee	beeline	belay
Belgium	belie	bellboy	below
Benjamin	Beulah	biennial	biology
blow	blue jay	Bohemian	baloney
Bombay	bonanza	bounteous	bowling
buffalo	Bulova	bungalow	byline

The bellboy went to Belgium.

Beulah plays the banjo.

The balcony was by the bay.

calmly	cameo	camouflage	Canada
cannonade	canoe	canopy	canyon
casino	casually	catalogue	cautiously
cavalcade	cello	chameleon	chancy
Chattanooga	chewing	Chicago	Chinatown
choosy	chow	Claudia	clientele
cloudy	cocoa	cola	coincide
collide	colloquial	colony	Columbia
comedy	company	confuse	congenial
cowhide	cozy	C.P.A.	Cuba

Send the catalogue to Chicago.

Claudia goes to Columbia.

What caused the cannonade?

D.A.	daily	dandelion	day
decoy	deeply	defy	delay
Delilah	delusion	denial	diagonal
dial	dialogue	diamond	Diana
dilemma	Dinah	dioxide	diva
doe	dogma	domino	Donna
double time	doughboy	dowdy	downsize
downtown	dubious	duel	
dungeon	duo	dynamo	

Donna wants the diamond.

I deny the dialogue.

It's the dilemma of the decade.

easily	ebony	ecology	ego
Eileen	Elena	elevation	eleven
Eli	Elijah	elusive	Emily
Emmanuel	empathize	emphysema	employee
enchilada	endive	enemy	enigma
enthusiasm	Episcopalian	epitomize	enjoy
envy	equalize	Eugene	
eventide	evil-eyed	encyclopedia	
eulogy	euthanasia	Eva	

We enjoy the employee.

I envy Emily.

Eli has an ego.

fade away	fallacy	family	Fay
F.B.I.	fee	feebly	fellow
fellowman	felony	fiancé	field day
fine	fivefold	flamboyant	flamingo
flow	flow in	flow out	flue
fluency	fly	flyaway	funny
foamy	folio	follow	
fountain	fume	fantasia	
fiasco	feeling	following	

I'll fly away with my fiancé.

Fay joins the family.

Follow the F.B.I.

gala	Galilee	galvanize	gaudy
geisha	gelatin	Geneva	genius
geology	ghostly	G.I.	gigolo
glassy	global	gloomy	glue
go	go along	goofy	gown
guillotine	gumbo	guy	gymnasium
getaway	gummy	golden	genuine

The gala is in Geneva.

He's a genius in geology.

Go with the gigolo.

Halloween	hallowed	handyman	hello
he-man	hideaway	highland	hobo
holiday	hollow	homely	honey
honeymoon	household	how	howling

hue	Hugo	humanize	hyena
heavenly	helium	hallelujah	hazy
hexagon	heehaw	hayseed	hullabaloo

The honeymoon was heavenly.

Say hello to Hugo.

Have a happy holiday.

Idaho	ideal	idealize	ideology
idolize	Illinois	India	Indiana
inflow	insomnia	inviolate	iodine
iota	I.O.U.	Iowa	I.Q.
Isaiah	island	ivy	Indonesia
ionize	icy	icon	inside

There's ivy on the island.

I owe you iodine.

Isaiah has insomnia.

Jamaica	Jane	Javanese	jaw
jawbone	jealousy	jelly	Jenny
jewel	Joan	Joe	Joel
joining	jolly	Josephine	jovial
joy	joyous	jubilee	juicy
Julia	June	juvenile	jam
javelin	Joshua	Jasmine	Japanese

Joan is jovial.

Jane lives in Jamaica.

Joe was born in June.

Katie	keynote	khaki	killjoy
kimono	kneeling	know	know-how
knowingly	K.O.	kowtow	kindly
kilo	Kalamazoo	koala	kidney
kiwi	keyway	kazoo	Kelvin
Kellogg	Kennedy	king-sized	Kyoto

Katie is a killjoy.

We have the know-how.

The kimono is khaki.

lady	llama	landing	landlady
laughing	lava	law	layman
lazy	lee	leeway	legion
lemonade	Lena	lenient	Leo
Leona	liaison	lie	likely
Lima	lime	limelight	limousine
linoleum	Lionel	Lisa	lively
localize	loin	lone	lonely
lonesome	looming	loudly	Louisiana
love	lovely	low	loyalty
lullaby	lumbago	Lydia	lousy
lagoon	logo	locomotive	lily

Lisa was lazy.

When is Leo landing?

I love lemonade.

madam	magnolia	mahogany	Maiden Lane
mainland	mainly	majesty	mammalian
mandolin	manual	matinee	maybe

May Day	meadow	mean	meaningful
meanwhile	medallion	medium	mellow
melody	Miami	Mikado	Milwaukee
mine	minimum	moan	modeling
mole-eyed	mollify	Mona	Monday
money	Mongolian	monotone	Montana
Montezuma	moody	mosquito	movie
mow	mow down	mule	mummy
museum	mutiny	manly	memento

Mona's in the meadow.

Play the melody for Monica.

There's money in Miami.

Naomi	Napoleon	navy	navy blue
needy	negligee	neophyte	nephew
Nevada	new	nullify	nylon
newly	nightgown	nightingale	Nina
nine	ninefold	no	Noah
nobleman	nobody	noisy	no one
no man's land	nostalgia	nosy	novelize
Novocaine	now	nowadays	no way
nucleus	notify	nosedive	

Nobody notified the navy.

Naomi needs Novocaine.

My nephew is nosy.

oblong	obvious	O.D.	oily
okay	Oklahoma	oleo	Olympian
Omaha	one	onion	on-line

only	ontology	oozy	openly
Ophelia	outflow	outlaw	outline
owe	ozone	obligation	odyssey
obscene	occasional	osmosis	oppose

Ophelia spoke openly.

We oppose the outline.

It's okay in Omaha.

pacify	Pamela	pantomime	Pasadena
Paula	paw	pay	payday
peeling	peewee	penalty	pendulum
Pentagon	psychology	Philadelphia	philosophy
phobia	photo	photophobia	physiology
piano	pie	pile	pillow
pine	pine cone	plasma	plateau
play	playboy	playland	plea
pleading	plenty	pliancy	plow
poison	pole	policy	polio
pony	posy	potato	phenomenon
pseudo	psycho	psychoanalyze	

Payday is May Day.

Pamela plays the piano.

Pay no penalty.

quail	qualify	quality	qualm
quantity	quantum	quasi	queasy
queen	questioning	quietly	
quota	quiz	quinine	

I qualify for the quota.

Send quinine to the queen.

Is it quality or quantity?

salami	San Diego	saw	saxophone
say	scandalize	Scandinavia	schedule
schoolboy	sea	sea lion	seasoning
seven	shadow	Shah	shallow
shining	shoe	show	shy
Siamese	sigh	sighing	skyline
slaying	slowly	sly	smile
smoky	snow	snowbound	socialize
solely	solo	someone	sonata
Sonia	son-in-law	spellbound	spy
stadium	stagy	stamina	stony
stowaway	studio	Sunday	sundown
swallow	Sylvia	symphony	

Let's go to San Diego.

Sylvia saw the show.

Buy a soda at the stadium.

taboo	tango	tapioca	tea
teatime	telephone	tidy	tiling
T.N.T.	toe	Toledo	tomato
tomboy	too	tooling	totem pole
tow away	towline	toy	toyland
tuba	T.V.	twenty-one	twilight
tympani	toboggan	tabloid	
tombstone	tailbone	tom-tom	
Taiwan	timing	titanium	

Tony's on the telephone.

In Taiwan, the tango is taboo.

We had tea for two.

U-boat	uneasy	unemployed	ungodly
unify	union	unity	unknown
unlawful	unveiling	unyielding	usually
Utica	utopia	utilize	ukulele
unison	U.F.O.	Uganda	ultimatum
unicycle	utensil	unanimous	
uncivilized	uneasy	uneven	
uncommon	uncoil	unavoidable	

Usually we unify.

The union is unyielding.

He's unemployed in Utica.

vacuum	valentine	value	vanity
Vaseline	veiling	velvety	Venus
veto	via	view	viola
violation	violin	visa	vocalize
vodka	volcano	vow	vanilla
valley	vista	visual	Vatican
vandalize	venue	video	viable
vine	vitamin	voyage	
vowel	vitality	volume	
volleyball	voodoo	vaudeville	

Be my valentine.

The video needs volume.

I vow to vocalize.

wanton	wavy	welcome	well done
wholesale	willow	wine	wise guy
woe	woo	wooing	Wyoming
whining	Washington	wallaby	wallow
washable	wangle	window	William
Wilmington	womanize	walkie-talkie	wall-to-wall
wagon	wail	walkway	waiting game

Welcome the wine.

Wyoming has willow.

The sign says "wholesale only."

Yankee	yawn	yawning	yea
yellow	Yellowstone	yielding	Y.M.C.A.
yoga	you	youthful	yowling
yo-yo	Yugoslavia	yuletide	yodeling
yoo-hoo	yuppie	yummy	Yolanda

Yolanda is yawning.

The Yankees play in Yellowstone.

Stay youthful with yoga.

Zambia	zany	zeal	Zealand
Zena	Ziegfeld	zigzag	zillion
zing	Zion	ZIP code	zodiac
zombie	zone	zonetime	
zoology	zoom	zucchini	
Zimbabwe	Zulu	zoo	

Ziegfeld is a zombie.

Zena loves zucchini.

Use ZIP codes for zones.

APPLYING WHAT YOU'VE LEARNED TO EVERYDAY SPEECH

Now that you've read over the practice words and sentences, make a conscious effort to apply what you've learned to your everyday speech. Relaxing the mouth, throat, and jaw, opening up your vowels, and being aware of resonance as you speak will all help to enrich the quality of your voice. Also, it's a good idea to practice reading out loud. Just about any material will do. Try poems, novels, short stories (if you have young children, use children's stories), even newspaper or magazine articles (especially editorials and advertisements) work nicely. Remember, just 10–15 minutes a day of voice-building exercises can produce dramatic results. So have fun working out and enjoy your new voice!

How to Put an End to Voice Strain and Ensure Consistent Vocal Strength

Just days before the 1992 presidential election, Bill Clinton's voice was so hoarse from laryngitis that he was forced to severely curtail his verbal attacks on George Bush to save what little voice he had left. Things got so bad that on one occasion, when his voice was too weak to continue, Hillary Clinton had to step in at the last minute to complete her husband's campaign speech.

You don't have to be out pounding the campaign trail to risk straining your voice. If your job requires you to raise your voice or talk for extended periods of time, even on the telephone, you could run into some trouble. Learn how to use your voice correctly now, so you can avoid problems later.

AVOIDING THE SIX MOST COMMON CAUSES OF VOICE STRAIN

The voice is a very delicate and vulnerable instrument and needs to be handled with care. Unfortunately, many speakers misuse the voice and end up hurting it. Here are six of the most common causes of voice strain, and how to handle them.

Avoid Yelling, Screaming, and Shouting

Shouting pushes sound through a tense throat and can strain the throat muscles. This can lead to all kinds of trouble, ranging from a sore throat to laryngitis. Your voice can't handle this kind of abuse for very long. Speaking with a relaxed throat, as well as using exercises to strengthen the voice, will enable you to get the maximum amount of sound with the least amount of effort. So the next time you're at a sporting event, think twice before yelling your guts out, especially if the following day is a work day. Besides, what team wants a cheering crowd of hoarse fans?

How to Speak in Noisy Surroundings Without Straining Your Voice

Crowded restaurants, noisy offices, airplanes, and even air conditioners can all make it difficult to judge the carrying power of the voice. As a result, many speakers overcompensate and end up pushing their voices beyond their limits. The more you push, the less sound you get in return. This is because a forced sound doesn't project as well as a free sound. If you have to speak under adverse conditions, concentrate on feeling resonance in the head and chest areas. When you're able to experience resonance vibrations as you speak, you've reached your optimal level of sound. Staying within your sound limit is one of the best ways to prevent strain.

Keep in mind that your ears aren't the only vehicle for judging sound; just because you can't hear your own voice doesn't necessarily mean you're not projecting. No matter what the external conditions may be, you can always trust the "inner feel" of your voice. Developing a "sense of sound" means you'll never have to strain to make yourself heard. Remember, *feeling* is believing.

How to Avoid Strain Caused by Forced Delivery

Speakers who use a high-powered, aggressive speaking style often wind up shouting at their audience. This can hurt the voice as well as the ears of the listeners. (Very loud voices tend to grate on people's nerves.) Make sure, therefore, that your voice can handle your speaking style. Listen to your body. If you suffer from frequent sore throats or hoarseness after speaking, chances are you're overdoing it. The remedy is simple: Save your voice and remember the rule, "Less is more." This is especially true when you're using a speakerphone, by the way. If you do a lot of talking into a speakerphone make sure you don't shout into it, just speak normally. The microphone is sensitive enough that your listener should be able to hear you just fine.

Avoid Using Unnatural Pitch

In an effort to sound more authoritative, many speakers, especially women, try to lower the pitch of their voices. However, forcing the voice down unnaturally for any length of time strains the throat muscles and can make you hoarse. Even worse, a listener can usually sense when a person is forcing out an unnaturally low pitch. Expanding your voice range is a gradual process and requires a fair amount of patience. There are really no quick fixes. With time and regular practice, you should get the results you want. Then, once your voice is properly developed, it will handle any reasonable demands you put on it. Be aware that building resonance into a voice can make it sound richer and deeper without actually being lower in pitch.

Refrain from Excessive Voice Use

Many speakers complain of fatigue and strain in their voices after extended periods of talking. This is especially true of people who spend a lot of time on the telephone. An untrained voice may show signs of fatigue well before the work day is over. This can cause a noticeable change in the *quality* of your voice. As a voice tires, it begins to weaken. Your sound can lose its vitality and energy, resulting in a much less convincing delivery. Vocal exercises to build strength and endurance will help your voice last longer, and prevent it from sounding tired. This means that towards the end of a long, hard day, you'll have the stamina to carry you through in top form.

How Harmful Irritants Can Cause Vocal Strain

While you know that inhaling cigarette smoke and consuming excessive amounts of liquor can be hazardous to your health, you may be unaware of the harmful effects these irritants can have on your voice. For example, did you know that heavy smokers and drinkers are more prone to chronic laryngitis than those who don't smoke or drink? Smoking also shortens your breath supply, limits your vocal range, and can interfere with the clarity of your overall sound. That's why so many smokers have raspy voices. Breathing certain chemicals may cause hoarseness and voice loss as well.

Even such a seemingly trivial habit as constantly clearing your throat can damage your vocal cords. In fact, vigorous throat clearing can cause *nodes*, a condition where lumps form on the vocal cords. In most cases, these will disappear as you develop good vocal habits. Keep in mind that clearing your throat can also be very irritating to your listener. There's nothing more annoying than being in the middle of a conversation and hearing a loud, scratchy, "GRRRRRUMPH"; it really can disrupt the flow of things. So the next time you feel the urge to clear your throat, resist and swallow instead. This is much better for your vocal tract and it won't distract your listener. (Be aware that there are certain phlegm-producing foods, too—dairy products in particular. It's a good idea to avoid consuming a lot of milk, cheese, or chocolate right before you have to speak. This way you'll have fewer interruptions.)

HOW TO HANDLE LARYNGITIS TO AVOID FURTHER VOCAL DAMAGE

Laryngitis occurs when the vocal cords become inflamed and swollen. It can make you sound hoarse or cause you to lose your voice altogether. Laryngitis can be brought on by a variety of factors, including viruses, excessive voice use, or heavy smoking and drinking. Resting the voice is usually the most effective cure. In most cases, you should have your full voice back within a few days' time. If your laryngitis lasts for more than two or three days or you suffer from persistent sore throat or hoarseness, you should see a doctor.

There are a few things you can do to prevent laryngitis from getting any worse. Obviously, the best solution would be not to talk at all. But, if you must talk, use your voice sparingly. Some throat specialists believe that whispering can actually put more strain on the vocal cords than speaking full out. So regardless of what kind of sound comes out, try to speak normally. If your throat is sore, drinking warm liquids such as diluted lemon juice and honey and using throat lozenges can have a soothing effect. Inhaling steam is also helpful. Try to avoid decongestants and antihistamines, which can dry out your throat. In general, a dry throat is more prone to infection, so drink plenty of non-alcoholic and non-caffeinated fluids to help keep the throat well lubricated.

ESTABLISHING GOOD VOCAL HABITS TO PREVENT THROAT PROBLEMS

Remember, developing good vocal habits can help prevent throat trouble in the first place. To keep your voice in good working order:

- Refrain from shouting.
- Don't constantly clear your throat, swallow instead.
- Avoid talking over loud noise whenever possible.
- Speak with a relaxed throat and concentrate on feeling resonance.

Learning to use your voice in a healthy way can help you overcome most throat problems.

Say It Out Loud!

Here are six brief quotations that you can read aloud (and/or memorize to say aloud without reading) as a way to practice what you've learned in this chapter. Use your full voice and concentrate on feeling resonance in each phase.

We love the free enterprise system. We live in a system where the making of a profit is ethically legitimized because the consumer is rewarded with better value. Yes, I love it if they call me a predator for those reasons.

Wolfgang Schmitt,
quoted in Seth Lubove, "Okay, Call Me a Predator," *Forbes* Magazine, February 15, 1993, p. 153.

'The bottom line is that people are judging your will, your capability to deliver.' It's a cliché but true: Weakness invites aggression.

PAUL WOLFOWITZ,
in Howard Banks, "Parkinson's Law Revisited," *Forbes* Magazine, August 15, 1994, p. 83.

Why do women have such a hard time breaking through to the top? E. Pendleton James, former head of personnel for the Reagan White House, points to a process he calls "BOGSAT—A Bunch of Guys Sitting Around a Table . . ."

NEHAMA JACOBS AND SARAH HARDESTY,
"Corporate Brides, Is It Worth It?" *Management Digest*, November 1988, p. S–5.

TQM (Total Quality Management) asks not how a business can spend less or make more, but challenges it to improve workers' relationships with one another and with management. . . . TQM assumes that all workers are already doing their best and that quality rests on an organized and positive work environment.

KRISTIE PERRY,
"What Worked for Japan Could Work for You," *Medical Economics*, October 25, 1993, p. 87.

We now know that the human being is a learning machine, and the problem is not to motivate people but to keep from turning them off.

PETER DRUCKER,
quoted in Elizabeth Hall, "A Conversation with Peter F. Drucker," *Psychology Today*, December 1982, p. 63.

A zero-sum game means my gain must be your loss. Poker and football games are zero-sum games. So is war, and so is a fight for market share.

BARRY NALEBUFF,
quoted in Rita Koselka, "Businessman's Dilemma," *Forbes* Magazine, October 11, 1993, p. 108.

7

How to Build a Voice That Grabs—and Holds—Attention to Get Your Message Across

HOW A POWERFUL DELIVERY CAN ACHIEVE BETTER RESULTS THAN STRONG CONTENT

When Phyllis Cadry joined the excited group in the hotel lobby, she was curious. "Hey, Frank," she asked, "what's all the fuss? Did I miss something?"

"You didn't miss Brett's *speech*, I hope!" Frank Scofield stared at her, his eyebrows climbing.

"No . . . I heard him," she said hesitantly.

"Then you know what we're all so wound *up* about! I tell you. I hear a lot of speeches—we all do, right? And most of the time I wonder how I'm going to stay awake until it's over. But Brett's talk . . ." Frank shook his head slowly. "I don't have the words to describe it. It was . . ." He shrugged his shoulders, and spread his hands to indicate his helplessness.

"It was *superb*!" put in one of the others.

"Right!" Frank said. "That's close!"

Her colleagues sounded like a hive of bees, all carrying on about Brett Hake's speech; clearly, the "superb" judgment was unanimous. Phyllis listened to them for a minute, and then she turned away and headed for her room.

173

I don't get it, she thought. I gave a talk this morning, too, and I know I had more important things to say than *Brett* did! All he did was spout one cliché after another! How come they're not telling me that *my* speech was a masterpiece?

Getting People to Listen to You

You may have had this experience yourself. It *hurts*. It hurts to put together a speech with solid content and give it your best delivery—and then watch some other speaker, who didn't work nearly as hard as you did, get all the glory. When this happens, whether you were talking to just one person or to hundreds, you can be about 99% certain that the reason is the two voices involved: Yours, and the one that grabbed and held everyone's attention so powerfully that they couldn't find words to express their admiration. The good news is, you too can have a voice like that; just follow the program in this book.

Obviously, your first objective as a speaker is to get people to listen to you. Without mastering this crucial first step, you'll never get any further. After all, before you can motivate, convince, or persuade, you must first have your listener's ear! As basic as this may sound, for many speakers it's a real struggle; they just can't grab and hold the attention of their audience. As a voice and speech coach, I've attended my share of business presentations and speeches, observing speakers as well as listeners. From what I've witnessed, most speakers are lucky if they can get half their audience to pay close attention to what they're saying.

An executive from a major publishing company came to me because he was having trouble motivating his people during weekly staff meetings. He complained that he never got the enthusiastic response he wanted. He even tried hiring a speech writer to help out. But no matter how compelling his message was, it always seemed to fall on deaf ears, not to mention sleepy eyes.

During our first coaching session, I asked him to try out part of his presentation. Towards the end of his short talk, even I found myself struggling to pay attention. The problem was clear: Here was a case of the dreaded *monotone*. He actually had some interesting points to make, but nothing stood out. His drab tone made everything sound the same. The whole impact of his message was lost.

Does this mean that most people are monotonous? Not exactly. The fact is, nobody really speaks in a monotone. Monotone literally means one tone; for all intents and purposes, you'd have to be a robot to talk using one tone or pitch all the time, but some speakers come close!

Throughout my years of teaching I've noticed an interesting phenomenon. Many business professionals are actually more engaging speakers outside the work environment than they are on the job. When I ask a student to tape record his or her voice in casual conversation, say chatting with a friend over the phone, I can often hear a good deal of color and expression in the voice. But if I listen to a recording of the same person in a business situation, say during a business presentation or meeting, much of the color and vitality often gets lost. The tone becomes flat and the person sounds like a dreadful bore.

Just Tell the Story

A partner at a major accounting firm was speaking at a national convention. He was highly respected as a leader but often dreaded as a speaker. At his best, he was monotonous. At his worst, well, let's just say he wasn't nicknamed "Johnny-one-note" for nothing. He was not the sort of speaker people looked forward to hearing—and judging by the audience reaction, this speech wasn't going to be any exception. But about three quarters of the way through his talk, something happened. He started to tell a personal story. The tone of his voice suddenly changed. His flat, lifeless delivery was gone and replaced with vibrant color and enthusiasm. For the first time he sounded like a coach motivating his team. Unfortunately, as soon as he finished his story, he slipped right back into the dreary monotone as he summarized the key points of his presentation.

When we reviewed the videotape of his presentation together, he witnessed the transformation and said, "If I could get the same passion and excitement I had in my story into the rest of my speech, they'd be eating out of my hands!" He was right on target. The solution was simple; I told him to think of his entire talk as one big "story." After all, just like a story, a speech has a beginning, middle, and end. It describes thoughts, feelings, and events to interest the listener. A good storyteller is able to captivate an audience by painting a picture with his or her voice. Think about the amount of color and variety you use when reading a story to a child. The next time you have a speaking engagement coming up, think of "telling a story" rather than "giving a speech." Go through your talk point by point and ask yourself, "What's the story?" Find the key elements and then, applying the techniques you learn in this chapter, use your voice to bring them to life.

Oddly enough, many business professionals confuse a flat speech pattern with authoritative speaking. In an attempt to sound more "professional" and businesslike, they get stuck in that dry, wooden, "execuspeech" pattern where the voice becomes devoid of all passion and emotion. They mistakenly believe that adding color and expression to the voice will make them sound too "theatrical," something that is taboo in the buttoned-up business world. Unfortunately, the end result is that when they give a lengthy talk, their flat tone produces a droning effect that too often leaves listeners in dreamland. Also, many women executives who force their voices down in an effort to get a deeper, more authoritative tone often wind up sounding monotonous.

Let's get one thing straight: You can't command authority if you can't command attention. Now, I know what you're thinking. Doesn't an authoritative voice automatically command attention? Yes, but only for a minute or two. Authority is the power to command, influence, or persuade. You can't influence or persuade people if they stop listening when you've hardly begun speaking.

HOW VOCAL VARIETY CAN INCREASE YOUR LISTENERS' INTEREST

What does the ear need to hear to stay tuned? Imagine you are listening to two different melodies, melody A and melody B. Say both melodies are the same length, but melody A has only four different notes while melody B has 12 different notes. Which melody do you think would be more interesting to listen to? The answer is melody B, of course. Why? Because melody B has more *variety*. Your speech works in much the same way. The voice with the most color and variety is the best attention-grabber.

How to Add Variety to Your Voice

Most of us do vary our voices to a certain degree. The key difference is that monotonous speakers sound boring because there's not *enough* variety in the voice. So, to liven up your delivery you're going to have to speak with a greater assortment of "notes." In speech terms this variation is known as *modulation* or *inflection*. Increasing it will help you sound more convincing and persuasive. And if you're concerned that adding color and variety to your voice will make you sound "theatrical" and unbusinesslike, don't be. A well-modulated voice will actually make you sound more committed to what you're saying.

Giving Your Message a Greater Impact

I recently had to watch a videotape of a top executive delivering a major presentation. If it hadn't been for the bullet points on his flip chart, I would have had a hard time figuring out what key points he was trying to get across. Everything came out sounding the same.

Whether it be a presentation, meeting, or phone call, the key points of your message have to stand out. To do this, the words you want to emphasize need special treatment. Modulating the voice on important words by raising or lowering the pitch highlights them just as italics do in print. Each person's voice has low, middle, and high notes or pitches. Sing "Happy Birthday" and you'll hear how the pitch of your voice goes up and down. When you talk, the pitch of your voice travels up and down as well. To speak with more color and variety, you simply need to increase the amount of pitch change on certain words.

HOW TO EMPHASIZE THE KEY POINTS IN YOUR MESSAGE TO KEEP YOUR LISTENERS' INTEREST

The most dramatic pitch change should occur on the most important words of your message—the words that best help to convey your point.

To a certain degree, that will depend on what exactly it is you're trying to say. Nonetheless, there are some general guidelines that can help.

As a rule, words that qualify or describe something, such as adjectives and adverbs, are good words on which to modulate. Sometimes emphasizing nouns and verbs, especially action verbs, works well too.

Raising the Pitch on Key Words for Emphasis

One effective technique to increase the impact of your message is raising the pitch of the voice on important words. For example, the inflection pattern for the statement "We have a *unique* opportunity" might look something like this:

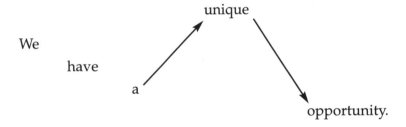

Notice how the pitch goes way up on the key word "unique" and then ends down on the final word "opportunity." Say this sentence out loud and tape record it. Make sure the pitch of your voice shoots up high on the key word "unique." If you're not used to speaking with a lot of inflection, you'll really need to exaggerate the amount of pitch change to get the desired effect.

In the following examples, let your voice rise quickly on the underlined words. Use a tape recorder to monitor your inflection pattern.

We want you to be <u>completely</u> satisfied.

They use an <u>innovative</u> approach.

This meeting is <u>extremely</u> important.

It's a <u>complex</u> and <u>sensitive</u> issue.

The <u>management</u> will make that decision.

Better <u>teamwork</u> is the answer.

You have to focus on <u>quality</u> and <u>productivity</u>.

They want to <u>encourage</u> diversity.

We need to <u>research</u> and <u>develop</u> new technology.

She's trying to <u>control</u> spending, not <u>increase</u> it.

Dropping the Pitch on Key Words for Emphasis

On the other hand, you can make the key points of your message stand out by dropping your voice *down* on important words. This helps to give more weight to your message. For example, using the "drop down" technique, the sentence, "She *wants* that promotion" might look something like this:

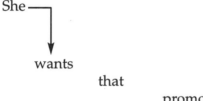

She
wants
    that
        promotion.

Say this sentence out loud and tape record it. Make sure your voice really drops down on the key word "wants." Keep in mind that you have to start high enough, so you have enough room left to make a dramatic drop in pitch. In the following sentences, drop the pitch of your voice down on each underlined word.

I can't <u>comment</u> on that.

This <u>never</u> should have happened.

You have to <u>earn</u> our trust.

They <u>know</u> it was a mistake.

He always <u>respected</u> you.

Whether you raise or lower the pitch isn't what matters: *changing* the pitch is what counts. It's the difference between being a dull or dynamic speaker.

AVOIDING INFLECTION TROUBLE SPOTS

Sometimes, even good speakers can lose their luster if they're not careful. Here are some special situations to watch for when the voice tends to get flat.

How to Read a List Effectively

It's easy to lapse into a monotone when running down a list of items. Too often, speakers sound as if they're reading off a shopping list when they list particulars. To avoid a flat delivery, vary the pitch of your voice on each item. For example, the inflection pattern of the statement "We have offices in New York, L.A., Chicago, and Dallas" might look something like this:

```
We                                          Chicago,
     have              New York,
        offices                                  and
              in
                            L.A.,
                                              Dallas.
```

Notice how the pitch changes on each city. It doesn't matter which item goes up or down, as long as you keep the pitch jumping. Say the above sentence out loud and tape record it, making sure you do something a little different with your voice as you say each item. Remember, modulating the voice on key items helps listeners better retain important information.

In the following examples, vary the pitch of your voice on each underlined word, using a tape recorder to monitor your inflection pattern.

We're accepting applications for <u>sales</u>, <u>marketing</u>, <u>accounting</u>, and <u>banking</u> positions.

She speaks <u>French</u>, <u>Spanish</u>, <u>German</u>, and <u>English</u>.

They offer <u>history</u>, <u>math</u>, <u>science</u>, <u>law</u>, and <u>economics</u> courses.

How to Recite Numbers Effectively

Numbers can sound extremely dry and dull if they're not handled properly. Situations where financial figures are quoted, such as annual shareholder meetings, don't have to be a crashing bore if you use a lot of inflection. Changing pitch on key figures also makes it easier for listeners to compare and contrast information. Observe the inflection pattern for the statement "Profits increased by 5% in 1997, 10% in 1998, and 15% in 1999."

```
                                                      15%
                                     10%              in
              increased             in      and      1999.
 Profits                  5%                1998
                     by        in
                          1997,
```

Say this sentence out loud and tape record it, making sure you're changing pitch on each figure.

Change the pitch of your voice on each number and/or item in the following sentences:

The new ad campaign will cost between <u>$50</u> and <u>$75</u> million.

Of the <u>1000</u> people surveyed, <u>55%</u> said they <u>drive</u>, <u>42%</u> said they use <u>public transportation</u> and <u>3%</u> said they <u>walk</u> to work.

We fly to over <u>20 countries</u> in <u>4 continents</u>, <u>365</u> days a year.

Overcoming Fatigue to Hold Your Listeners' Interest

Picture this. You're taking the "red-eye" flight from Los Angeles back to New York. You're putting in 60-hour workweeks, you have jet lag and you're low on sleep. Add to this the fact that you have a very important meeting to attend shortly after you land. You feel exhausted—and if you're not careful, you're going to sound exhausted, too.

A grueling work schedule can take a toll on your body as well as your voice. When you're rundown, your body's energy level drops and so does the energy level of your voice. The amount of color and variety in your voice usually diminishes when you're tired, causing your voice to become flat. This can make your message sound a lot less convincing. Extreme fatigue can even make an otherwise dynamic speaker sound lifeless. So when you're running low on steam, make an extra effort to keep that voice jumping as you speak! This way, even though you may feel wiped out, you'll still have vocal vitality.

Keeping the Interest in Repeated Presentations

If you have to give the same presentation over and over again, your delivery can start to sound stale. This is especially true of people who sell over the telephone. Their mechanical delivery makes them sound as if they're reading their sales pitch to prospects, which can turn a listener off within a matter of seconds. So how do you make a boring routine sound interesting?

Think of Broadway actors who must recite the same lines night after night, week after week, month after month, and in some cases year after year! With ticket prices as high as $100 a seat, their performances better not sound stale! How do they do it? Well, they sort of make a game out of it. For one thing, they use tons of inflection. They also experiment with different inflection patterns so no two performances sound exactly the same. If they can do it, so can you. Remember, when you're bored, it's easy to lapse into a monotone. Modulating the voice is a great way to make your speech sound fresh and spontaneous. After all, *you* know it's the hundredth time, but your *audience* shouldn't know.

Presenting Technical Material Effectively

Pay attention to inflection if your talk involves specialized or complicated language. Many speakers think they sound impressive when they use technical terms. The truth is, jargon can sound extremely dull if it's not presented with enough variety. Handle complex material with lots of inflection.

I recently coached an executive at a top accounting firm who had to give a presentation regarding some new tax legislation. At one point, as I tried to get him to spruce up his delivery, he stopped short and said, "Hey, come on, there's only so much I can do with this kind of material." Dead wrong. Never blame your subject matter for your boring presentation. No matter how dry the material may seem, it's your job as a speaker to make it sound interesting.

Taming the Rising Inflection Syndrome

When you make a statement, does it sound like you're asking a question? I recently tried to call an executive at her office and was told by her assistant, "She's in a meeting right now?" This response left me wondering, "Are you asking me or telling me?" While some Irish and English dialects often end statements with a rise in pitch, this speech pattern is not a part of Standard American English. Nonetheless, this habit seems to be reaching epidemic proportions in this country. It can be heard in just about all dialects affecting men and women of all ages, especially those under 35. The fact is, that in Standard American speech, pitch that rises at the end of a phrase or sentence indicates a question, and a question indicates uncertainty. When you're asking for something or need information, a questioning tone is perfectly acceptable. However, using a rising pitch pattern at the end of a statement takes the authority and conviction out of your message. It makes you sound tentative and weak.

There should be a clear difference between the sound of a question and a statement. As a rule, the final word of a statement should drop *down* in pitch. For example, the statement "We need to hire four directors" should look something like this:

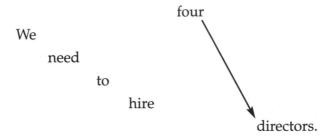

Dropping down on the final word, "directors," makes a declarative statement. It tells the listener that you know what you're talking about. To take the uncertainty out of your speech and put the confidence and assertiveness in, make sure you end your statements with a drop in pitch. It's the difference between sounding sure or insecure. Record yourself whenever possible to monitor your inflection pattern.

VARYING THE RHYTHM OF YOUR SPEECH TO INCREASE YOUR LISTENERS' INTEREST

While changing the pitch of your voice on key words is a very effective attention-grabbing technique, it's not the only one. Another way to increase the interest of listeners is by varying the rhythm of your speech.

What is *rhythm*? Rhythm involves the duration of sound. In music, long and short notes are grouped together in different patterns that create rhythmic variety. In speech, rhythm refers to the amount of time you take to say your words.

What to Do If the Rhythm of Your Speech Is Too Regular

Listening to words spoken in a uniform pattern is about as interesting as listening to a ticking clock. To avoid a mechanical delivery, you need to vary your rhythm as well as your pitch.

How Slowing Down Key Words Gives Them Importance

Slowing down on important words gives them more weight and significance. In the following sentence, notice how the first three words get stretched out to create additional emphasis.

"N-O O-T-H-E-R C-O-M-P-A-N-Y has this technology."

Say this sentence out loud and record it. Make sure you are slowing down on "No other company."

Take extra time to emphasize the elongated words in the following sentences.

There's only o-n-e m-o-r-e t-h-i-n-g we can do.

E-V-E-R-Y-B-O-D-Y needs to get involved.

We noticed a s-i-g-n-i-f-i-c-a-n-t d-i-f-f-e-r-e-n-c-e in their management style.

Only a-u-t-h-o-r-i-z-e-d p-e-r-s-o-n-n-e-l can enter.

We provide the h-i-g-h-e-s-t l-e-v-e-l of service.

She has an u-n-u-s-u-a-l a-b-i-l-i-t-y to bring people together.

USING THE PAUSE TO CREATE INTEREST IN YOUR SPEECH

What makes the opening of Beethoven's Fifth Symphony so exciting? It's the rests (moments of silence) in the music that actually create much of the drama. Pauses in your speech can have the same kind of dramatic effect. Would the immortal words of our great leaders have the same impact without the pause? Judge for yourself. Here are two well-known quotations from Neil Armstrong and Franklin Delano Roosevelt. First say each statement from beginning to end, without pausing.

Then repeat the same statement, adding the pause. If you have a tape recorder handy, record yourself.

"One small step for man—one giant leap for mankind."

NEIL ARMSTRONG

"The only thing we have to fear—is fear itself."

FRANKLIN DELANO ROOSEVELT

I think you'll agree that adding the pause makes those statements sound much more powerful and dramatic. But for a lot of speakers, even a second or two of silence in the middle of a thought can seem like a long time and make them feel uncomfortable. The fact is, pauses make up a vital part of your speech pattern and shouldn't be neglected. Pausing from time to time allows you to think your ideas through and gives listeners a chance to absorb what you say. When used carefully, pauses can also hold the attention of your audience. They can increase the curiosity of your listener. This all happens in a second or two, but can be very effective.

Practice observing the pauses in the following sentences. Double slash marks are used to indicate pauses:

If I hear another word // the deal is off.

When we say reliable // we mean reliable.

The issue is not about wages // it's about job security.

Our policy is // the customer is always right.

Remember that there's a lot of power in a little pause. You don't have to fill the airwaves all the time.

Tips to Practice Your Speech

If you're speaking from a written text, here are a few visual aids that can help:

- Underline the important words of your talk with a colored marker to remind you which words need a dramatic pitch change. You can also use italics to signify key words.

- Indicate where you want to take extra time by e-l-o-n-g-a-t-i-n-g key words with dashes. Slowing down can also be indicated with an arrow below the key word. It might look like this:

   I absolutely believe in this plan.

   ⟵————————

- Write in double slash marks // to signify pauses.
- Once you've marked your text, go back and read your entire talk out loud. Use a tape recorder to monitor yourself and make sure you observe all your markings.

You will be amazed at how much the techniques described in this chapter will do to make *you* a speaker whose voice keeps listeners hanging on your every word. With the strength and the power you've been adding to your voice from the very beginning of this book, plus the information you've just learned, you won't have to stand by while people rave about somebody else's speech. *You'll* be the one getting all the compliments.

Say It Out Loud!

Here are seven brief quotations that you can read aloud (and/or memorize to say aloud without reading) as a way to practice what you've learned in this chapter. Vary the pitch and rhythm of your speech and use pauses to make your delivery sound convincing.

All politicians say as little as they can. Only the very greatest can get away with saying nothing. Abraham Lincoln in his 1860 campaign did not make a single speech . . .

GARRY WILLS,
"Hurrah for Politicians," *Harper's* Magazine, September 1975, p. 46.

Agriculture helps farmers steal from workers and businesses; Commerce helps businesses steal from farmers and workers; and Labor helps workers steal from farmers and businesses. With a plan to abolish all three, you could promise every American that he was losing one friend and two enemies.

STEVEN E. LANDSBURG,
"Rational Explanations: The Sins of the Grandfathers," *Forbes* Magazine, February 13, 1995, p. 85.

In today's tough TV competition, it is not so important how many people watch a network's programs. What matters is whether viewers are the kind of people who buy advertisers' products. The ratings make the headlines, but it is the demographics that advertisers buy.

SUBRATA N. CHAKRAVARTY,
"The Ratings Game," *Forbes* Magazine, October 1, 1990, p. 43.

It used to be that most companies looked after their own word processing, payroll, security, travel, legal, accounting, and cafeteria needs. No more. By farming out these tasks to specialists, corporations are saving time and money and can pay more attention to their core businesses.

KATE BOHNER,
"Business Services and Supplies," *Forbes* Magazine, January 3, 1994, p. 108.

Politicians have many virtues that ignorant people take for vices. The principal ones are: 1) compromise of principle; 2) egoism; 3) mediocrity. In other men these may be vices; but for a politician they are needed skills . . .

GARRY WILLS,
"Hurrah for Politicians," *Harper's* Magazine, September 1975, p. 45.

It's like you say on Wall Street: Bears make money, bulls make money, but hogs get eaten.

TERRY EHRICH,
quoted in Jerry Flint, "Publisher's Heaven," *Forbes* Magazine,
November 12, 1990, p. 78.

Are chief executives worth the big paychecks they often draw? Among the ones who do earn their keep—and more—are those chief executives who succeed in taking a troubled company and restoring it to health. In doing so they may save thousands of jobs . . .

REED ABELSON ET AL.,
"Corporate Leaders: Is There a Doctor in the House?," *Forbes* Magazine, May 28, 1990, p. 218.

Part 3

Using Your New Vocal Advantage to Reach Your Goals

8

Improving Your Grammar and Usage to Sound Smooth and Seamless

HOW POOR GRAMMAR CAN UNDERMINE A COMPANY'S REPUTATION

"Wasn't that something?" Larry Grange asked the other two men as they stepped out of the elevator at the restaurant and got in line. "Can you believe that? I mean, why doesn't somebody *tell* the guy, for crying out loud?"

John Holt nodded. "It doesn't make any sense to me. Why would a company like Megamax spend a fortune training somebody like that and sending him around the country to sell their product? Why not just set fire to their money and save themselves all that time and effort?"

"Did I really hear him say, 'Our company don't produce second rate homes' or did I imagine that?" Clyde Campbell put in.

"You didn't imagine it, Clyde. I heard it, too."

"Me, too! And twice I heard him say something had 'growed' in the past six months. *Growed!*"

The hostess signaled that she had a table free for them, and they followed her into the dining room, but they didn't drop the subject; it was too good to drop. It had been so amazing, listening to the man from Megamax murdering the English language . . . they were going to have stories to tell about *this* turkey for years to come!

"The guy may have something going for him that isn't obvious," Larry said as they sat down and opened their menus, "but it sure isn't *brains*!"

Clyde chuckled. "It's going to make it a lot easier to plow Megamax under," he pointed out. "We should all be *grateful* to the guy!"

"Right," John agreed. "Let's just hope nobody wakes up and sends him back to school!"

DON'T GET CAUGHT IN THE POOR GRAMMAR TRAP

This is a sad situation. The three men in the above scenario are biased, and they're quite wrong. There is no evidence whatsoever that people who don't speak Standard English are less intelligent than people who do. The man they're making such cruel fun of may be intelligent and capable and competent; he may be someone of great value to his company. But unfortunately, the way they've perceived him is the way almost *everybody* will perceive him. No matter what the actual facts are, he will be judged less than bright and less than competent, on the basis of his grammar and usage.

You can't afford to get caught in this trap. No matter how much you have improved your voice, if you use it to speak in a manner that others consider uneducated, crude, perhaps even stupid, you are throwing away your chances for success. In this chapter we will consider the steps you can take to be sure that doesn't happen to you.

Reviewing Grammar to Prevent
Embarrassing Situations

If you're like most people, you'd probably rather undergo a root canal than study grammar and usage. It's no wonder. The topic conjures up memories of a laundry list of complex rules and confusing terminology that you were forced to learn back in grade school. Well, let me put you at ease. This is not a grammar course. We will bypass the tedious exercises and instead focus on the most common mistakes or "bloopers" in spoken English. We all can remember the acute embarrassment caused by using the wrong word at the wrong time. The goal here is to make sure it doesn't happen again.

Why is a little grammar and usage refresher important? Because, quite simply, people judge you by those two factors. In addition to the sound of your voice, people form an opinion about you based on your command of the English language. The kinds of words you choose to use and how you put them together can make you sound very professional and polished. On the other hand, poor use of language can tarnish your image and derail your career.

Every effort has been made here to remove the pain and suffering and make the information as simple and easy to learn as possible. This section presents the most glaring errors and embarrassing mistakes that speakers usually make. You'll learn what to say and what not to say. With just a little bit of practice and repetition you'll be amazed at how you can break your bad habits and make your speech "blooper-free."

Common Verb Errors to Avoid

PRESENT TENSE PROBLEMS TO SOLVE

Some speakers forget to add "s" when they use the third person singular of regular verbs. For example, a person might say, "She *direct* the sales force" instead of "She *directs* the sales force."

The third person singular (the form that goes with "he, she, it," or a singular noun) is the only one that adds "s" to the verb.

>*Don't say:* Management *give* the orders.
>
>*Say:* Management *gives* the orders.

When the subject is singular, the verb must be singular as well. If the subject is "managers" (a plural noun), then "give" would be correct, as in "The managers *give* the orders."

>*Don't say:* He *try* to be helpful.
>
>*Say:* He *tries* to be helpful.

Don't say: Most of the time it *work* well.

Say: Most of the time it *works* well.

Don't say: The company *expect* to see profits rise.

Say: The company *expects* to see profits rise.

Don't say: This issue *deserve* more attention.

Say: This issue *deserves* more attention.

"Don't" and "Doesn't" Problems

Sometimes "don't" and "doesn't" are confused and people make the mistake of using "don't" with *he, she,* or *it.*

Don't say: She *don't* speak English.

Say: She *doesn't* speak English.

Don't say: It *don't* matter.

Say: It *doesn't* matter.

PAST TENSE PROBLEMS TO SOLVE

Some speakers drop the "ed" endings of past tense verbs. For example, a person might say, "He *talk* with them yesterday" instead of "He *talked* with them yesterday."

Interestingly, people often add "ed" endings when they write, but drop them when they speak. Make sure you clearly pronounce all "ed" past tense endings.

Don't say: They finally *convince* me.

Say: They finally *convinced* me.

Don't say: She never *expect* us to be there.

Say: She never *expected* us to be there.

Don't say: It *happen* at the worst time.

Say: It *happened* at the worst time.

AVOID IRREGULAR VERB PROBLEMS

Sometimes a verb doesn't simply need "ed" to form the past tense. Instead, the verb may change drastically. For example, the past tense of "strike" is "struck." This is known as an irregular verb. For your convenience, a list of the most common irregular verbs can be found at the end of this chapter. See the ones with which you need to familiarize yourself. Keep in mind that even well-educated speakers confuse some of the trickier irregular verbs from time to time.

Sometimes you may know that a verb is irregular but you simply use the wrong form.

Don't say: I *seen* it.

Say: I *saw* it.

Don't say: You *done* it.

Say: You *did* it.

When "have" or "has" comes before the main verb, you must use the *past participle* form. For example, "They *have* already *begun* the meeting." When "have" or "has" isn't present, simply use the past tense form. For example, "They *began* the meeting on time."

Don't say: If I had *knew* about it before, I would have called you.

Say: If I had *known* about it before, I would have called you.

Don't say: The company has *grew* tremendously.

Say: The company has *grown* tremendously.

Don't say: They've never *wrote* us.

Say: They've never *written* us.

Don't say: I've never *rode* on a horse before.

Say: I've never *ridden* on a horse before.

Don't say: He has already *took* his vacation.

Say: He has already *taken* his vacation.

Don't say: We've *wore* out our welcome.

Say: We've *worn* out our welcome.

Don't say: She has *spoke* very highly of you.

Say: She has *spoken* very highly of you.

Don't say: I would have *did* it differently.

Say: I would have *done* it differently.

PROBLEMS WITH "BE" TO AVOID

Watch out for the present and past tense forms of the verb "to be." Some speakers use "is" and "was" even when the subject is plural.

Don't say: The books *is* on the table.

Say: The books *are* on the table.

Don't say: They *was* downtown.

Say: They *were* downtown.

Here's a handy breakdown on the present and past tense forms.

Present

I am   we/you/they are
you are
he/she/it is

Past

I was   we/you/they were
you were
he/she/it was

Don't say: We *was* just about to leave.

Say: We *were* just about to leave.

Don't say: The bottles *is* in the truck.

Say: The bottles *are* in the truck.

Don't say: You *was* out to lunch.

Say: You *were* out to lunch.

Making Verbs and Subjects Agree So You Will Always Sound Literate

On a recent train ride to Philadelphia, I heard the conductor make an announcement about the train's on-board telephone. He ended by saying, "Instructions for using this phone is located at the side of the phone."

Why? Presumably because he didn't realize that the subject of his sentence was "instructions" rather than "phone." He should have said, "Instructions for using this phone *are* located at the side of the phone." (It's also possible that he was following the rules of his own nonstandard dialect; not all dialects agree on this rule.) Most of the people listening to him came to negative conclusions about his education and/or intelligence because of that mistake.

The rule the conductor broke was the one which says that subjects and verbs must *agree* in number. That is, plural subjects take plural verbs; singular subjects take singular verbs. Most of the time that rule is easy to follow, but there are a few patterns of English that cause confusion. Should you say "His collection of recordings *is* impressive" or "His collection of recordings *are* impressive"? Should you say "A stack of papers *is* on my desk" or "A stack of papers *are* on my desk"? Should you say "The media *is* too critical of politicians" or "The media *are* too critical of politicians"? Should you say "The staff *is* working on the project" or "The staff *are* working on the project"? The answers to these questions involve four different factors; let's take them up one at a time.

USING CLASSIFIERS CORRECTLY

When you studied the English "parts of speech," you probably didn't learn anything about *classifiers*. That's because classifiers are a very limited phenomenon in English today. You use them all the time, however. When you say "a herd of horses" or "a flock of crows" the words "herd" and "flock" are classifiers. All you have to remember is that when the subject of your sentence is "an X of Ys" your verb must agree in number (singular or plural) with X. You say "A herd of horses is in the field" and "Two herds of horses are in the field"; the verb must match "herd" or "herds." And phrases like "a bunch of bananas" or "a collection of records" follow this rule, which is very reliable.

There are sequences that look like this pattern but are actually quite different. For example: "A Princess of the Isles walked by" or "A house of bricks was built beside the road." Don't worry about it. For both of these, the verb will still have to agree with the part before "of."

Using "Either" or "None" Properly

It's very common for people—even speakers of Standard English—to say "None of the answers are right." That's wrong, strictly speaking. "None of . . ." (and "either of, each of, another of," and so on) work just like the classifier patterns. You say "None of the answers is right" and

"Either of the answers is acceptable." It will help to remember that if you're dealing with one of these you can always insert the word "one." For example: "Either one of the answers"; "Another one of the pitchers"; "Each one of the children." And "none" is just an alternate form of "not one." Since "one" is always singular, the verb must be singular too.

Solving the "Committee" and "Clergy" Puzzle

There is a list of common words for which verb agreement is sometimes puzzling. It includes "committee, staff, clergy, group, team, jury, family" and any other word before which you could insert "A member of the . . . The members of the . . . ." Usage for these words varies. You will find one handbook that insists on "The clergy is in the chapel" and another that says only "The clergy are in the chapel" can be used. You need to follow the rule that your teacher or boss or other authority figure wants you to follow. When you don't know what to do, put in "member of/members of" and follow the rule for classifiers.

Using the Correct Forms of Foreign and Scholarly Words

To get the subject/verb agreement right for words like "media, alumnae, cacti, criteria," you have only one choice of strategy: you just have to learn them one at a time. These are almost always words from the scholarly vocabulary, usually from Latin or Greek. As a rough guide, you should remember that "a" and "us" are singular endings, while "ia," "ae," and "i" are plural ones. So you would say "The media are too critical" but "The alumnus is refusing to make a donation."

Solving Problems with Pronouns to Speak Correctly

Using the incorrect pronoun gives the impression that you are a careless speaker, or worse, uneducated. This can immediately turn off listeners so they disregard the message. Make sure you are not using the wrong pronoun.

EIGHT COMMON PRONOUN CONFUSIONS

Here are eight common confusing misuses that need correction:

Eliminating the "Me" and "I" Confusion

Do you ever start off a sentence with "me"? If so, you shouldn't. Use "I" when it's the subject of a sentence. For example:

Don't say: Me and Michael attended the conference.

Say: Michael and *I* attended the conference.

Here's a handy tip: take away one of the subjects (Michael) and try out the same sentence. "*Me* attended the conference" is wrong, but "*I* attended the conference" is right. Also, notice the order. It's not "I and Michael attended the conference," but "Michael and I attended the conference." Always place yourself last.

Don't say: Me and him will go.

Say: He and *I* will go.

Using "Her," "She," "Him," "He" Correctly

The same rule applies to *he, she, we,* and *they.* Use these when they're one of the subjects of a sentence, or when they *identify* the subject.

Don't say: It was *me.*

Say: It was *I.* (Identifier)

Don't say: You and *her* can make the team.

Say: You and *she* can make the team.

"*Her* can make the team" is wrong, but "*She* can make the team" is right.

Don't say: You and *him* should do the research.

Say: You and *he* should do the research.

Using "Me" Correctly

Not to worry. There's still a place for little old "me." Use "me" when it's *not* the subject of your sentence.

Don't say: He spoke to Bob and *I*.

Say: He spoke to Bob and *me*.

Once again, take away "Bob" and try out the sentence. "He spoke to *I*" is wrong, but "He spoke to *me*" is right.

Don't say: Thanks for asking Bill and *I* to join you.

Say: Thanks for asking Bill and *me* to join you.

The same rule applies to *him*, *her*, *us*, and *them*. Use these only when they're *not* one of the subjects of your sentence.

Don't say: It was for Laura and *she*.

Say: It was for Laura and *her*.

"It was for *she*" is wrong, but "It was for *her*" is right.

Avoiding Errors in Using "Myself," "I," and "Me"

Never use "myself" in place of "I" or "me."

Don't say: My wife and *myself* will attend.

Say: My wife and *I* will attend.

Take away the first half of each sentence and you're left with two choices: "*Myself* will attend" or "*I* will attend." I think you'll agree that "*I* will attend" is the hands-down winner.

Don't say: They drove Carol and *myself* to the office.

Say: They drove Carol and *me* to the office.

Take out "Carol and" to make the picture clearer. It's wrong to say "They drove *myself* to the office" but it's correct to say "They drove *me* to the office."

Whatever you do, don't use "me" in place of "myself." This is a major blooper and will immediately convey a lack of education to your listener.

Don't say: I bought *me* a new suit.

Say: I bought *myself* a new suit.

Dropping Nonstandard Forms from Your Vocabulary

Some speakers have picked up the bad habit of saying "hisself" instead of "himself" and "theirself" and "theirselves" instead of "themselves."

Don't say: He did it *hisself*.

Say: He did it *himself*.

Don't say: They made those *theirself*.

Say: They made those *themselves*.

Do yourself a favor; strike "hisself" and "theirself" from your vocabulary. These words are simply not part of Standard English vocabulary.

Using "Who" and "Whom" Correctly

Strict grammatical rules dictate that "who" should be used when it's the subject of a sentence as in "*Who* did all the work?" *Whom* should be used elsewhere, as in "Give this to *whomever* wants it." The fact is, "whom" is being heard less and less these days and really shows up more in writing than in speech. As a result, when you answer the phone it's okay to say, "*Who* do you wish to speak to?" Somehow, "To *whom* do you wish to speak?" sounds just a bit too stilted for today's speech patterns.

Eliminating the "Who" and "That" Confusion

For many speakers, a little less of *that* and a little more of *who* would be a good thing. Here are a couple of simple rules you can use to clear up any confusion.

- Use *that* when you want to refer to a thing.
- Use *who* when you want to refer to a person.

Don't say: The man *that* answered the phone was extremely rude.

Say: The man *who* answered the phone was extremely rude.

Don't say: The women *that* won the award were all Harvard graduates.

Say: The women *who* won the award were all Harvard graduates.

Clearing Up "Them" and "Those" Questions

To clear up any possible confusion, all you need to remember is that "them" is a non-subject pronoun and can never come right before a noun.

Don't say: Let me have some of *them* cookies.

Say: Let me have some of *those* cookies.

Other Common Speech Problems
That Need Solving

Here are common speech problems that detract from the message and leave listeners with an unfavorable impression. Be sure to avoid these problems:

ELIMINATING DOUBLE NEGATIVES

Two wrongs don't make a right, but two negatives do make a positive. Negatives include words such as *no, nothing, can't, never,* and so on. Using two negatives in the same statement is not allowed in Standard English and may distort the meaning. Double negatives very quickly will run up a red flag suggesting that you are poorly educated and unqualified for any leadership position.

> *Don't say:* I didn't see *nobody.*
>
> *Say:* I didn't see *anybody.*

> *Don't say:* We couldn't go *nowhere.*
>
> *Say:* We couldn't go *anywhere.*

> *Don't say:* She *ain't got no* money.
>
> *Say:* She *doesn't have any* money.

> *Don't say:* Nothing was *never* said to me.
>
> *Say:* Nothing was *ever* said to me.

KNOWING WHEN NOT TO USE "MORE" AND "MOST"
WITH ADJECTIVES

I once overheard a manager say to one of his employees, "You're more *stupider* than I thought." If only he knew just how stupid *he* sounded!

The rule is simple: Never use *more* before an adjective that ends in "er" and never use *most* before an adjective that ends in "est." For example:

Don't say: This is *more* easier.

Say: This is *easier.*

Don't say: He's the *most laziest* person I know.

Say: He's the *laziest* person I know.

Here's another rule worth remembering:
In most cases, if an adjective has more than two syllables, don't add "er" or "est," use "more" instead. For example:

Don't say: She is *beautifuler* than the rest.

Say: She is *more beautiful* than the rest.

Don't say: This is *difficulter* than the other project.

Say: This is *more difficult* than the other project.

ELIMINATING THE EXTRA "AT"

This has to be one of the most glaring errors today. Too many speakers use "at" where it doesn't belong.

Don't say: Where are you *at?*

Say: Where are you?

Don't say: I don't know where Bill is *at.*

Say: I don't know where Bill is.

It's okay to say "I can be reached *at* home," but it's wrong to say "Where can I reach you *at?*" Just say, "Where can I reach you?" To create a good impression, never use *at* to end a sentence.

HOW TO PHRASE QUESTIONS CORRECTLY

In some dialects of English it's okay to ask an indirect question with the same word order that you use in direct questions. Standard English doesn't allow that, however. Here are the patterns:

Standard English:

Direct question:	What time is the party?
Indirect question:	I wonder what time the party is.

Nonstandard English:

Direct question:	What time is the party?
Indirect question:	I wonder what time is the party.

The nonstandard form is more regular; nevertheless, the rule for Standard English is the safer choice and will make a better impression on others.

Avoid Using Wrong Words That Can Cause Embarrassment

Have you ever been embarrassed when someone points out that you've used the wrong word? If this happens to you on occasion, it may be because there are certain pairs of words that sound very similar but actually mean something very different. Imagine the trouble you could get into confusing a *sensuous* dinner, which pleases the senses, with a *sensual* dinner which implies sexuality. If you learn the meaning differences for these words, you can avoid potentially embarrassing situations.

EIGHTEEN COMMONLY MISUSED WORDS THAT NEED CORRECTING

The following words are often used incorrectly. As you go through this list, see which words you need to brush up on.

Lay vs. Lie

What's the difference?

Lay means to place something down. You *lay* something somewhere. *Lie* means to recline or rest somewhere. You can't *lie* something. Something *lies* by itself. (*Lie* as in "to lie down" is not the same as *lie* as in "to tell a lie." These are two different verbs, with two different past tense forms.)

Don't say: I need to *lay* down for a while.

Say: I need to *lie* down for a while.

Don't say: *Lie* the papers on the desk.

Say: *Lay* the papers on the desk.

Be careful: The past tense form of lie is not lied or laid, but lay!

Don't say: Yesterday, I *lied* down on the couch.

Say: Yesterday, I *lay* down on the couch.

Raise vs. Rise

What's the difference?

Raise means to lift or bring up. You can raise something. Raise is always followed by an object as in "I raised my hand."

Rise means to move from a lower to a higher position. You can't rise something. Something rises by itself. For example, "The sun rises at six o'clock."

Don't say: They *rose* the ceiling.

Say: They *raised* the ceiling.

Set vs. Sit

What's the difference?

Set means to place in a position. You set something somewhere.

Sit means to lie or rest. You can't sit something somewhere.

Don't say: He *sat* the toolbox on the bench.

Say: He *set* the toolbox on the bench.

Don't say: I *set* down.

Say: I *sat* down and I *sit* down.

Good vs. Well

What's the difference?

Good is an adjective. It is used to modify or describe a noun as in "She's a good teacher."

Well is an adverb. It is used to modify or describe a verb as in "He speaks well."

Don't say: She sings very *good.*

Say: She sings very *well.*

Lend vs. Loan

What's the difference?

Strictly speaking, *lend* is supposed to be a verb and *loan* is supposed to be a noun. For example, you *lend* someone a hammer but someone needs a *loan.* However, in everyday conversation it's now considered acceptable to use *loan* as a verb. But there is one important distinction that a lot of speakers fail to make: *loan* should be used for physical transactions such as money or goods.

Don't say: Can you *lend* me $200?

Say: Can you *loan* me $200?

Don't say: *Loan* us your support.

Say: *Lend* us your support.

Anxious vs. Eager

What's the difference?
Use *anxious* when you're actually worried about something.
Use *eager* when you're looking forward to something.

Don't say: I'm *anxious* to start my vacation.

Say: I'm *eager* to start my vacation.

Bring vs. Take

What's the difference?
Use *bring* when something is carried toward the speaker.
Use *take* when something is carried away from the speaker.

Don't say: *Bring* these slides to Ellen.

Say: *Take* these slides to Ellen.

Don't say: You'd better *bring* that suitcase over there.

Say: You'd better *take* that suitcase over there.

Amount vs. Number

What's the difference?
Use *amount* when you're talking about quantity.
Use *number* when the things you're talking about can actually be counted.

Don't say: They had a large *amount* of offices in the East.

Say: They had a large *number* of offices in the East.

Fewer vs. Less

What's the difference?
Use *fewer* when you're talking about things that can be counted.

Use *less* when you're talking about an amount or quantity as in "I make a little *less* money now."

Don't say: He has *less* accounts than she does.

Say: He has *fewer* accounts than she does.

Farther vs. Further

What's the difference?
Use *farther* when you're talking about physical distance.
Use *further* when you can't measure physical distance.

Don't say: We can't go any *further* on this road.

Say: We can't go any *farther* on this road.

Don't say: I must know my schedule *farther* in advance.

Say: I must know my schedule *further* in advance.

Continual vs. Continuous

Continual refers to something that goes on frequently but with occasional interruption.
Continuous refers to something that goes on without interruption.

Don't say: He was *continuously* asking questions throughout my presentation.

Say: He was *continually* asking questions throughout my presentation.

Don't say: The car alarm rang *continually* for thirty minutes.

Say: The car alarm rang *continuously* for thirty minutes.

Imply vs. Infer

Imply means to suggest. A speaker implies something.
Infer means to draw a conclusion. A listener infers something.

Don't say: I didn't mean to *infer* that you were cheating.

Say: I didn't mean to *imply* that you were cheating.

Don't say: Because of my response, she *implied* that I was upset.

Say: Because of my response, she *inferred* that I was upset.

Learn vs. Teach

The key point to remember is that you learn *from* someone or something but someone teaches something *to* you.

Don't say: I'm going to *learn* you some manners.

Say: I'm going to *teach* you some manners.

(Of course, it's correct to say "You should learn some manners.")

Like vs. As

As a rule, it's okay to use "like" after words such as "seem," "sound," "feel," "taste," "look," and so on. For example, "It sounds *like* they need some help" would be considered acceptable usage in most speaking situations. However, in the following example "as" should be used instead of "like."

Don't say: *Like* I was saying, I'm originally from New York.

Say: *As* I was saying, I'm originally from New York.

Way vs. Ways

Remember, "way" is singular and "ways" is plural. Don't use "ways" when you need the singular form.

Don't say: We're a long *ways* from home.

Say: We're a long *way* from home.

Easy vs. Easily

What's the difference?
Easy is an adjective. It needs to modify a noun.
Easily is an adverb. It needs to modify a verb or an adjective.

Don't say: He was able to sell the house *easy*.

Say: He was able to sell the house *easily*.

Real vs. Really

Use *real* when you want to describe a noun, as in "a real problem." Use *really* when you want to describe a verb or adjective.

Don't say: We thought they did a *real* good job.

Say: We thought they did a *really* good job.

In this case, *really* describes the adjective *good*.

More Unique vs. Unique

Unique means "the only one of its kind." It can't be modified.

Don't say: This is the *most* unique formula.

Say: This formula is unique.

NONSTANDARD WORDS TO DROP FROM YOUR VOCABULARY

The following nonstandard words should never be used.

Somewhere vs. Somewheres

Avoid using "somewheres" instead of "somewhere."

Don't say: It must be *somewheres* around here.

Say: It must be *somewhere* around here.

Adding an "s" to *somewhere* certainly isn't going to help your career.

You vs. Youse and You-all/Y'all

"You" refers to one person or a group of people.
"Youse" and "you-all/y'all" don't exist in Standard English.

Don't say: All of *youse* can fit in the van.

Say: All of *you* can fit in the van.

Regardless vs. Irregardless

People sometimes believe that "irregardless" is a more formal way of saying "regardless." Actually, "irregardless" is nonstandard usage. It's better to use "regardless" instead.

Don't say: Irregardless of his exhaustion, he continues to work 14-hour days.

Say: Regardless of his exhaustion, he continues to work 14-hour days.

Using Irregular Verbs Correctly to Enhance Your Speech

The following verbs tend to give speakers the most trouble; the principal parts of each verb are listed as well. Remember, when "have" or "had" comes before the main verb, use the past participle form, as in "I have begun" or "I had begun."

Present	*Past*	*Past Participle*
arise	arose	arisen
awake	awoke/awaked	awoke/awaked
bear	bore	borne/born
beat	beat	beaten/beat
become	became	become
begin	began	begun
bend	bent	bent
bet	bet	bet
bid (offer)	bid	bid
bid (command)	bade	bidden
bind	bound	bound
bite	bit	bit/bitten
bleed	bled	bled
blow	blew	blown
break	broke	broken
bring	brought	brought
build	built	built
burst	burst	burst
buy	bought	bought
cast	cast	cast
catch	caught	caught
choose	chose	chosen

Present	Past	Past Participle
cling	clung	clung
come	came	come
cost	cost	cost
creep	crept	crept
cut	cut	cut
deal	dealt	dealt
dig	dug	dug
dive	dived/dove	dived
do	did	done
draw	drew	drawn
drink	drank	drunk
drive	drove	driven
eat	ate	eaten
fall	fell	fallen
feed	fed	fed
feel	felt	felt
fight	fought	fought
find	found	found
fling	flung	flung
fly	flew	flown
forbid	forbade	forbidden
forget	forgot	forgotten/forgot
forgive	forgave	forgiven
freeze	froze	frozen
get	got	gotten/got
give	gave	given
go	went	gone
grind	ground	ground
grow	grew	grown

Present	Past	Past Participle
hang (suspend)	hung	hung
hang (execute)	hanged	hanged
have	had	had
hear	heard	heard
hide	hid	hidden
hit	hit	hit
hold	held	held
hurt	hurt	hurt
keep	kept	kept
know	knew	known
lay (place)	laid	laid
lead	led	led
leave	left	left
lend	lent	lent
let	let	let
lie (recline)	lay	lain
light	lighted/lit	lighted/lit
lose	lost	lost
make	made	made
mean	meant	meant
meet	met	met
pay	paid	paid
prove	proved	proved/proven
put	put	put
quit	quit	quit
read	read	read
ride	rode	ridden
ring	rang	rung
rise	rose	risen

Present	Past	Past Participle
run	ran	run
say	said	said
see	saw	seen
seek	sought	sought
sell	sold	sold
send	sent	sent
set	set	set
shake	shook	shaken
shine	shone	shone
shoot	shot	shot
show	showed	shown/showed
shrink	shrank/shrunk	shrunk/shrunken
shut	shut	shut
sing	sang	sung
sink	sank	sunk
sit	sat	sat
sleep	slept	slept
slide	slid	slid
slit	slit	slit
speak	spoke	spoken
speed	sped	sped
spend	spent	spent
spin	spun	spun
split	split	split
spread	spread	spread
spring	sprang/sprung	sprung
stand	stood	stood
steal	stole	stolen
stick	stuck	stuck

Present	Past	Past Participle
sting	stung	stung
strike	struck	struck
string	strung	strung
swear	swore	sworn
sweat	sweat/sweated	sweated
sweep	swept	swept
swim	swam	swum
swing	swung	swung
take	took	taken
teach	taught	taught
tear	tore	torn
tell	told	told
think	thought	thought
throw	threw	thrown
wake	woke/waked	woken/waked
wear	wore	worn
weave	wove	woven
wed	wed	wed
weep	wept	wept
wet	wet/wetted	wet/wetted
win	won	won
wind	wound	wound
wring	wrung	wrung
write	wrote	written

Now, that wasn't so bad, was it? Just a little bit of practice and repetition can rid your speech of those embarrassing misused words. In a very short time you'll have the added polish and professionalism that will help you move ahead in today's competitive world.

9

Overcoming the Fear of Public Speaking to Sound Confident and Poised

HOW THE FEAR OF PUBLIC SPEAKING CAN PREVENT YOU FROM ADVANCING IN YOUR CAREER

When Susan Weed got home from work, she was delighted to see that her husband was already there. And when Harvey handed her a cocktail and motioned for her to sit down, she was even more pleased. "They offered you the job!" she said. "Terrific!"

"Yes, they offered me the job," he told her. "But no—it's not terrific."

"What do you mean? How can it not be terrific?"

Harvey looked at the floor. "I turned it down," he said.

"You *what*?" Susan couldn't believe her ears. "You're kidding! You turned down a seven thousand dollar raise? With stock options?"

"Yes, Susan, I did. I sure did."

She stared at him, but he was still avoiding her eyes. "*Why*?" she demanded. "I don't understand at all. I thought you *wanted* that promotion!"

"There was something I didn't know," he said.

"Like what?"

"Like nobody had mentioned to me that I'd have to be prepared to go out and give a bunch of speeches, Susan. If I'd known that was part of the job, I never would have asked to be considered for it."

"But, Harvey! You're intelligent and articulate and you know the business; you could—"

He raised one hand sharply, cutting her off, and interrupted with, "Stop! Please—just don't say another word."

"But—"

"I *mean* it! I would rather go work on the gutting line at the *poultry* plant than give even *one* speech! Public speaking scares me to death! And I'm not alone, either. Didn't you see that survey? People are more afraid of public speaking than they are of *dying*!"

He came over and sat down beside her then, and he put his arm gently around her shoulders. "Honey," he said, "I am truly sorry. I know the job would have been wonderful for us. But I have to turn it down, and you're going to have to forgive me. I *can't* make speeches . . . I just can't."

How to Handle Nervousness and Successfully Speak in Public

If you are someone who finds it easy to give talks and public presentations, you may find this scenario hard to believe. But if you're like many other people, you know that in Harvey Weed's place you would have done exactly the same thing he did. For you, the very thought of public speaking means a dry mouth, a rapid heartbeat, a knotted stomach, and trembling knees. It means stark *terror*.

It may comfort you to know that even some of the most experienced speakers get nervous. A well-known network TV weatherman was so stricken with stage fright that he reportedly would let out ear-piercing screams off-camera trying to calm himself down. He actually went as far as poking himself in the backside with a pin in an attempt to jolt the jitters out of his system. Others have resorted to drugs such as beta-blockers to cope with their fears. (While this may sound tempting to some, you should be aware that beta-blockers are a potentially dangerous group of drugs prescribed for heart patients that block the stimulating effect of adrenaline on the heart. Common side effects include lethargy and fatigue.)

Keep in mind that a drug can only mask physical symptoms of anxiety. No medication can help overcome the fear itself. Before you consider such drastic measures, consider this: a certain amount of nervousness can actually be beneficial. It can give you the extra edge and focused concentration to reach your peak level of performance. On the other hand, a high level of anxiety can interfere with this concentration and cause a speaker to lose control.

Most of us get nervous because we're afraid of making embarrassing mistakes in front of others. The root of this problem often lies in a lack of adequate preparation. Many people believe that they are prepared for a speaking engagement, yet when it comes time to address a group they become filled with terror. This may indicate that they are actually not as well prepared as they might think.

I want to caution you about a saying I've come across time and time again regarding public speaking. It goes something like this: "Think of public speaking as enlarged conversation." Admittedly, this statement can have a very comforting effect on an inexperienced speaker. It might well ease your phobia for the time being, but be careful. This way of thinking can sometimes do more harm than good.

Some people try to psych themselves into believing that public speaking is really no big deal; after all, it's just "enlarged conversation." As a result, they often don't put the necessary time and preparation into their talk and, when it comes time to face a group, they panic.

The fact is, speaking before a group is really not like conversation. Here are just a few of the differences:

A conversation involves an exchange of information, whereas most speaking engagements are a one-way affair. In a public speaking format props are often used (such as a flip chart, overheads, a podium, or a microphone) that are not part of ordinary conversation. There's also a sharp contrast in the way your audience responds. For example, the sound of one hundred people laughing at your opening joke is a very different experience from having one or two people chuckle during conversation.

In many ways, speaking before a group is a lot more like a performance. But don't let the word "performance" scare you. If you know how to prepare yourself, you're going to do just fine.

Four Steps to Build Confidence and Reduce Anxiety

Learning good rehearsal techniques is essential to build confidence and reduce anxiety. Here are a few simple steps to follow:

STEP 1: PLAN AHEAD

Start organizing your material as far in advance as possible. The more rehearsal time you give yourself, the more relaxed you will be. Procrastinating will only put unnecessary pressure on you. The professional actor, musician, or dancer would never consider performing without weeks or months of intense rehearsal. Yet many speakers think nothing of facing an audience after reading their speech through only a few times. No wonder public speaking is their number one fear!

STEP 2: PRACTICE OUT LOUD

Once your speech is written, read it aloud in full voice. If possible, tape your reading and listen to it. This will give you a sense of how the words actually sound. Many times written text takes on a new character when spoken out loud. You'll find that certain written language doesn't always translate well into speech, so edit when necessary. Make sure everything you've written is comfortable to say. Avoid using words that are hard for you to pronounce. "Keep it simple" is a reliable rule when you speak.

STEP 3: SIMULATE THE CONDITIONS OF YOUR SPEAKING ENVIRONMENT

If your presentation calls for visual aids such as a flip chart, overheads, or slides, use them when you rehearse as well. If you don't have access to any of these, use your imagination. Go through the motions of writing on a flip chart or pointing to a slide. This will allow you to get a sense of the action and will also help your timing.

If possible, try to rehearse in the room where your speech will actually take place. Getting acquainted with your speaking environment beforehand can really put you at ease during your presentation. If this isn't possible, once again, use the power of your imagination. Pretend that your office or living room is the conference room or auditorium where your speech will be delivered. As silly as it sounds, you can even practice your eye contact using objects such as chairs and pillows as make-believe people.

STEP 4: PRACTICE IN FRONT OF PEOPLE

For best results, rehearse your talk before a group. In the arts, this is known as the final dress rehearsal. Here, performers run through an entire show in costume before a small audience. It's usually the last chance to make any changes or corrections. This is an invaluable step of the rehearsal process that most speakers omit. To help conquer his stage fright, an executive I coach teaches a business course at a local university just for the practice of getting up and speaking in front of groups. You can seek out public speaking opportunities as well. For example, if you belong to a religious organization, volunteer to speak at your house of worship (read aloud from the holy books, and so forth). Join committees at your work place and give yourself practice by speaking out on important issues. Also, look for opportunities to speak in your community. Some possibilities may include your tenant association, your Parent Teacher Association, or fraternal clubs. Even proposing a toast at a dinner party is a good start. The more you speak in public, the easier it gets. Who knows, you might even start to enjoy it after awhile.

Whatever avenue you choose, one thing is certain; there's no substitute for a live audience. If you really want to conquer the fear of public speaking, you have to practice speaking in front of people. Start by inviting a few friends over to listen to your speech. Spread the chairs around to create the illusion of a large audience. The more factors you can familiarize yourself with before your speech, the more in control you'll be during your speech. The less you leave to chance, the better. You may even want to dress up for the occasion. If you think that all this is too embarrassing, ask yourself this question: Would you rather be embarrassed before your friends or before your colleagues? Friends are usually a lot more forgiving.

You'll probably be a little nervous even when addressing this sympathetic group. That's the idea. When you're nervous and under pressure, sometimes unexpected things can happen. For one thing, you may realize that you don't know your speech as well as you thought you did. Or maybe a section of your talk that went well when you practiced alone gave you some trouble in front of a group. This is what a rehearsal is *for*. It exposes your strengths and weaknesses in advance and allows you to make any corrections well ahead of time. Then, when the real day comes, you'll have a lot less to worry about.

Obviously, it's best to leave sufficient time between the dress rehearsal and the actual speaking date, in case you need to make any revisions in your material. And, of course, if you really "bomb out" on your first try you can always call a second dress rehearsal. You'll be amazed at the difference practicing before an audience can make. When the time comes to face your colleagues, you'll be spared that "first time terror" that many unprepared speakers experience, and you'll enjoy the confidence and relaxation that comes from being well rehearsed.

Additional Techniques to Help Control Nervousness When Speaking

Let's go back to those symptoms of anxiety that were mentioned earlier in this chapter: the dry mouth, rapid heartbeat, knotted stomach, and trembling knees. As bad as these may sound, there are actually a couple of other things that can go wrong when your nerves get the better of you. You may experience shortness of breath as well as a shaky voice. Here are some things you can do to help control these and other anxiety-producing symptoms.

USING BREATHING/RELAXATION EXERCISES TO LOOSEN UP

When you get nervous, your mouth, throat, and jaw often tighten up. A tight throat can disrupt your air flow and cause shallow breathing. This makes the voice sound thin and may cause quivering. To prevent this from happening, practice a series of easy breathing exercises before you speak. These exercises will relax the mouth, throat, and jaw and help you achieve better breath control.

1. Using the breath only, without sounding the voice, exhale on the syllable "PAAAAAAAAAAAHHHHHHHHHH." The aim is to make a long, sustained breath.

2. Breathe normally.

3. Let the jaw drop down and open the mouth wide. (Think of your mouth position when a doctor makes you say "AH" to examine your throat.)

4. Keep the mouth, throat, and jaw relaxed.

5. Allow the air to flow out evenly and stop as you begin to run out of breath. It should feel like a lazy yawn.

6. Repeat: "PAAAAAAAAAAAHHHHHHHHHH."

7. Following the same instructions, exhale on:

   "TAAAAAAAAAAAHHHHHHHHHH."

   "KAAAAAAAAAAAHHHHHHHHHH."

   "MAAAAAAAAAAAHHHHHHHHHH."

These easy breathing exercises are a good stress-reducer; because they're silent, they can be practiced just about anywhere. Doing a series of these right before you speak can really calm your nerves and help alleviate those last-minute jitters.

USING GESTURES EFFECTIVELY TO HELP CALM YOUR NERVES

Unfortunately, the feedback participants receive from typical public speaking/presentation skills programs often casts a negative light on gestures. With the arrival of the video camera we now can see every subtle movement we make and often the insignificant gestures are overanalyzed and blown out of proportion. The first thing that comes to a speaker's mind is "Oh God, I look so stupid!" Many people react by curtailing their movements and wind up as stiff as a board. Don't restrain yourself by thinking that you must keep your hands at your sides. While it's true that too many gestures can be distracting, a reasonable amount of hand and arm movement, especially during the opening moments of a talk, can help release excess tension from your body. This can do wonders for those trembling hands and knees. The point is not to choreograph your movements, but to allow your body to move freely and naturally.

HOW CONCENTRATING WILL HELP YOU AVOID NERVOUSNESS

Another way to help reduce anxiety is to become completely focused on what you're doing. If you're worrying about what others think of you, you're not fully concentrating on your job. Keep in mind that in most cases your audience really does want you to succeed. You can't be critic and performer at the same time! Try to channel your energy and emotions into your material. Get involved.

Many people become preoccupied when speaking in public and may suffer lapses in their concentration. Here's a good exercise that can help. (The aim is to purposely create an obstacle as you rehearse your talk to test your level of concentration.) As a challenge, the world renowned cellist, Pablo Casals, would alter his environment by practicing the cello in total darkness. You can do similar things as you rehearse. For example, try practicing part of your talk while standing on one leg. Next, close one eye (you can do this with one leg up or if that's too much for you, keep both feet on the floor) and continue a portion of your presentation. Then try *singing* the words to your speech. That's right, make a song out of it! If this all seems too ridiculous, don't worry; there's a method to this madness. Once you can get through your talk with all these obstacles, especially the singing technique, speaking normally even in front of a group will be a piece of cake! When it comes time to deliver your talk you'll be able to look your audience in the eye and say to yourself, "You can't make me nervous, I can present this material on one foot, closing one eye, and I can even *sing* it!" This is a great exercise to improve your concentration and boost your confidence as well.

PACING YOURSELF TO ENSURE CORRECT TIMING

Maintain a moderate pace. Nervousness can cause people to speak too fast. The opening of a talk is usually when a speaker's anxiety level is at its highest. Your body is charged up with a healthy dose of adrenaline and this can increase your tendency to rush through your speech. A bad case of nerves can distort your sense of timing. What feels like normal pacing to you may very well be much too fast for your audience. So make a point of starting out slowly and deliberately, and remember to pause for breaths as you speak. This will help you to stay in control. (To learn more about pacing, refer to Chapter Three.)

SPEAKING UP WILL BUILD CONFIDENCE

As you begin your talk, start out big and strong. Use your full voice, which will help prevent it from cracking or quivering. Save the subtleties for later on when you're more relaxed. Also, when you're nervous it's a good idea to speak in short phrases. Saying fewer words in each breath will give you better voice control and help get your words out with greater power and conviction. Remember that a well-trained voice will obey any reasonable demands put on it and work for you under all conditions, even when you're under pressure. In short, developing your voice will help take the worry out of your voice and put the confidence in.

Reviewing Confidence-Building Techniques

Here's a quick rundown of steps to follow to help you sound confident even when the pressure is on:

1. Do a series of long, relaxing breathing exercises:
   ("PAH-H-H-H-H-H," "TAH-H-H-H-H-H," and so on)
2. Use gestures freely
3. Concentrate on doing your job
4. Pace yourself
5. Pause for breaths as you speak
6. Rehearse! Rehearse! Rehearse!

Guidelines for Using a Microphone to Your Vocal Advantage

No question about it, speaking into a microphone causes many speakers to experience a great deal of unnecessary anxiety. A lot of this fear really comes from not having a clear understanding of how to use a microphone. We've all witnessed the unlucky speaker who starts speaking into a microphone only to realize that it's not turned on. Here are a few guidelines to help you prevent some of the most common microphone mishaps:

- Before you actually begin your speech into a microphone, make sure it is plugged in. Check for an on/off switch. The best way to test a microphone is to speak into it. Either count off a few numbers or just talk normally. Blowing into or tapping against a microphone can hurt the microphone as well as the ears of your audience.

- If possible, try to do a sound check in advance. Find a sound engineer or someone who has the expertise to help you. If you can't find anyone, you can adjust your volume by your proximity to the microphone. Start out about six inches away from the microphone and see how you do. If the sound is too loud, back away a little. On the other hand, if you're having a hard time being heard, you can move in a little closer. As a rule, a person with a loud voice should stand a bit farther away from a microphone than a person with a soft voice.

- Keep in mind that every microphone is different; some are more sensitive to sound than others. The key is learning to adjust your distance to the microphone to get the best sound. If you speak too close to a microphone your words may become fuzzy and garbled. This creates distortion. Speaking too close may also cause *feedback*, that dreaded high-pitched, ear-piercing noise that occurs when there's an overload of sound. After this happens, most listeners tend to forget what's being said and brace themselves for another assault on their eardrums. The problem is usually that the sound is too loud. If you run into feedback, back away a little.

- Be aware that when a sudden rush of air hits a microphone it can create a jarring sound for your listeners. So, if you have to cough, sneeze, or clear your throat, make sure you turn your head away from the microphone. These minute distractions can sound like thunder when they're amplified! Also, watch out for "popping p's." If you hear a tiny explosion every time you say the letter "p," adjust your position slightly. Don't talk directly into the microphone, talk across it instead, and try not to hold it with your hand.

- If you're not accustomed to using a microphone, having a piece of metal pointed towards your mouth can be a little intimidating. As with anything else, practicing is the best cure. To help you overcome this awkward feeling, try rehearsing your talk *with* a microphone. If you don't already have one, you can buy a small inexpensive microphone that hooks into a portable cassette player. Since hearing your voice amplified over a sound system for the first time may seem strange to you, rehearsing with a tape recorder will help you get used to hearing the sound of your voice when it's reproduced mechanically.

- Finally, don't think that a microphone is going to do all the work for you. All a microphone does is amplify sound. This means that if you have a nasal, shrill, or shaky voice, these traits will be significantly increased over the mike. As a rule, use a microphone only when the situation really demands it. Depending on the size and acoustics of the speaking environment, a well-developed voice will usually have enough carrying power to reach most small audiences without a microphone. When I was a graduate student at Juilliard, Herbert von Karajan, the conductor of the Berlin Philharmonic, led a master class at Alice Tully Hall. After being introduced by the president of Juilliard, Maestro von Karajan shoved the microphone aside, stood erect and proceeded to address the 1100-person audience directly. Even though he didn't have a particularly strong voice, he was still able to make himself heard. This may be an extreme example, but given the right conditions, there's nothing like relying on your own natural amplifying power to impress an audience.

Facing Your Audience with Confidence to Make Your Best Impression

One of the most common mistakes speakers make when using visual aids is that they talk to the visual aid and not to the audience. I once sat through a presentation where the speaker was using a flip chart. He had a lot of interesting points to make, but I couldn't hear a good portion of what he was saying because the ends of his sentences trailed off. After a while this became very frustrating. It wasn't that he ran out of breath at the end of his sentences; the problem was in how he used the flip chart. He would talk and write at the same time. Instead of completing his thought facing the audience, he would turn to write on the flip chart in the middle of a thought. Each time his face turned away from the audience, his words got lost.

The next time you use a blackboard, flip chart, slides, or overheads, make sure you finish what you want to say *facing your audience*; then turn to your visual aid. This will ensure that your listeners hear every word. Facing your audience as you speak also helps you maintain good eye contact.

The same rule applies when you speak from a written text. Don't look down at your notes until you've completed a thought or phrase. Remember, for your voice to project well, you must aim your sound directly at your audience.

Wrapping Up Your Fear of Public Speaking

There *are* some good reasons for being afraid when you have to give a speech. Suppose you don't have time to prepare the speech or rehearse it, and you're going to have to just "wing it." Suppose you have to talk about something you don't really understand very well. Suppose you know you're facing a truly hostile audience whose major goal will be to make you feel foolish. Suppose you've just had a bad case of the flu and you keep having uncontrollable coughing spells without any warning. Suppose you know from long experience that people find your voice unpleasant to listen to and hard to understand. In all those situations, you *should* be afraid—they're scary!

But most of the time people who are afraid to talk in public don't have good reasons of that kind. Most of the time their fear isn't rational. If you have prepared your speech carefully and rehearsed it adequately, if the circumstances of the occasion are the normal ordinary ones—and if you have followed the program in this book so that you have a pleasant, powerful, and compelling voice—you have absolutely no reason to be afraid. A little anxiety is natural and often helpful; you should expect it and welcome it. But *fear* of speaking will not be a problem for you any longer. Not with *your* vocal advantage.

Conclusion

Now that you've gone through this book, you should have a better understanding of what it takes to build a better voice. As you practice the drills and exercises, please remember to be patient with yourself. You may not always get the results you want the first time around. In fact, it's very common for a new student, after practicing the first week, to come back and say to me, "I think I'm getting worse. I hear myself making more mistakes now, than before I came here." Of course, this isn't the case at all. What's really happening is that the student is simply becoming more aware of his or her own voice. Unfortunately, the new student usually hears the "bad" things first and often misses all that is good in the voice. (As your awareness increases, you'll also hear the "good" and "bad" in other people's voices.)

Don't focus on the negative. Accept your imperfections for now and realize that no matter how bad you think you may sound, there's still a lot of good in your voice. The goal is to build on the strengths of your voice and by doing so you will overcome your weaknesses.

Remember, one of the main reasons you sound the way you do is because of speech habits you learned (consciously as well as unconsciously) throughout your life. You know that changing old habits takes time so don't get discouraged.

Think of your voice as an instrument. It takes a violinist a good 15 years of intensive daily practice to gain a solid command of the instrument. To get the most out of your voice you have to learn how to "play" your vocal instrument to the best of your ability. This won't happen overnight, but it will happen over time. The good news is that unlike a violinist, you won't need to practice six hours a day; you won't even need six hours each week. You'll find that just 10-15 minutes a day can produce dramatic results.

How long does it take to hear an improvement in your voice? The answer can range from several weeks to several months. It really depends on how far you want to go. It is my hope that you will have the desire and motivation to develop your speaking voice to its fullest potential and not be satisfied by meeting only the minimum standards. After all, the better you sound, the more options open up for you.

Remember, whether it's fair or not, you are judged by the way you sound and ultimately you are paid for the way you sound. If you think about it, there really is a bottom line connection to your voice. The better you speak, the greater your earning potential.

As stated in the very beginning of this book, improving your voice is the best investment you'll ever make. So keep working on it. As you strengthen and polish your voice, it will become your greatest asset. Use it well and make your fortune!

Appendix

Practice Speeches

Here's a collection of speeches that you can read aloud as a way to practice all the new skills you've learned in this book.

AN UNEVEN PLAYING FIELD IN AMERICA

Bernard Shaw, Principal Washington Anchor, CNN

The Alfred M. Landon Lecture on Public Issues, Kansas State University, Manhattan, Kansas, November 20, 1992. Used by permission.

The Center for Creative Leadership says on an average nine out of ten female managers are pushed into staff jobs such as human resources and public relations—positions that do not lead to the top of corporate America. If people are not given work experiences to broaden themselves, how can they ever get the opportunity to be more responsible?

Presently, fewer than 6 percent of all the top executives in the United States are female. This problem, this crisis, this scandal is exacerbated by a natural human tendency: to surround yourself with people like you. [Former] Labor Secretary Lynn Martin says, "If the person at the top is male and white, invariably he picks people around him who are just like him." And as this happens each day in our cities, each day in our counties, and each day in our states, each day we as a nation suffer. And when this great nation suffers, we lose another step in competition because we are failing to use fully our most precious talent and resource—our own people.

Federal, state, and local laws are there. But laws are given life and force by people and companies and universities willfully looking after their best interests, and, fortunately, that is happening. But it is happening too slowly. Some companies and some executives are acting with conscience to change the way the work place and society treat women. Some. Not a majority.

PASSPORTS—NOT PROVINCIALISM: MARKETERS AND COMMUNICATORS NEED NEW INTERNATIONAL SKILLS

Jean L. Farinelli, Chairman and Chief Executive Officer, Creamer Dickson Basford

Delivered to a joint meeting of the Charlotte World Trade Association and the Carolinas Chapter of the Business/Professional Advertising Association, Charlotte, North Carolina, April 14, 1993. Used by permission.

What I see happening today is this: World trade is expanding, but marketers and communicators are not keeping up with the pace. We still think of other countries as "foreign." We *know* that we do not know enough about "foreign" countries, so we fall back on what we *do know*—how to market and communicate in our *own* country. We repeat the slogan, "Think globally and act locally," but we do not really mean it. I am not speaking only of the United States—as my examples demonstrate, marketers and communicators from *many* countries lack the international skills they should have in order to be effective.

We have to realize that "international" is not "foreign" anymore. If we marketers and communicators are going to live and prosper in a world of international business, we must become *figurative citizens* of every country in which our companies operate. We need passports—not provincialism.

Companies that pursue international business need marketers and communicators who truly are *internationalists*. They need people who can help reinvent marketing and communications to meet global needs. They need marketers who can participate in the process of explaining global corporate strategies. They need communicators who can persuade senior managers to step outside of their familiar thought processes, in order to meet other cultures on their own terms. They need communicators who can articulate—simply and consistently—the outcomes of very complex global decisions.

THE CHALLENGE OF CHANGE: BUILDING A NEW COMPETITIVE SPIRIT FOR THE 21ST CENTURY

Ralph S. Larsen, Chairman and Chief Executive Officer, Johnson & Johnson

Delivered to the Executive Club of Chicago, October 23, 1992. Used by permission.

I am very optimistic about our future and I believe that our progress over the next few years will take us to the threshold of a new century, one which promises both unprecedented challenge and enormous hope. But it is critical that the badly strained fundamentals of this country work well once again. And for that to happen our basic business systems must perform both *competitively* in the world economy that will unite us and *compassionately* in addressing the social imbalances and economic grievances that threaten to divide us.

I think we would all agree that to have 37 million people without health insurance in a nation like ours is simply not right. But if we are going to deal with this and similar issues, we need to revolutionize and revitalize our public institutions. And we need to insist that they learn from and work cooperatively with the private sector so that the creation of wealth is not siphoned off by the size and inertia of an unresponsive bureaucracy.

Business *cannot* be a spectator on the sidelines of unfolding events. Neither can government and its institutions be oblivious to the signs that are so obvious—and so repugnant—to the people it serves. Clearly, we need to renew our competitive spirit, sharpen our focus, revitalize our institutions, and re-engage the great entrepreneurial drive that engineered America's once dominant leadership position.

In closing, may I say the tasks we face in both the private and public sectors will not be easy and it will take a nation of broad shoulders to make it work. But confronting the *challenge of change* is what created the supremacy of American enterprise in the first place, and, in the final analysis, it is what will help us regain that position, which is so critical to the future of this great nation.

THE CHANGING CONSUMER: PREDICTING THE MARKETPLACE OF THE FUTURE

Wendy Liebmann, President, WSL Strategic Retail

Delivered to the Drug Store of the Future Symposium, Tarpon Springs, Florida, January 14, 1992. Used by permission.

Picture it. Twenty-first century America. It will begin as an age of immigration. People will flock to these shores from Haiti and Cuba, from Mexico and China, from Hong Kong and Uzbekistan. Sometimes by choice. Often by necessity. Often through no free will of their own.

Arriving in their millions, they will land in Los Angeles, Seattle, Miami, and stay just where they land, in a ghetto-like community reminiscent of their homeland. Like their twentieth-century counterparts, they will come looking for the American dream. A chance to work for a living, to earn enough to feed their families, to practice their own religion, and hold their own political views—with no fear of persecution. They will come to be Americans, but different Americans, diverse Americans, maintaining a strong sense of their own heritage and the character of the land from which they came.

They will *not* assimilate as fast as they can learn the language. In fact, English will never be their primary language. They will be proud of their national tongue.

They will not cast off their foreign ways. They will not dress like Americans, eat like Americans, speak like Americans, live like Americans, as those of the twentieth century did. Instead they will retain the essence of their own distinctive culture.

And so will be born a new face for twenty-first century America. And so will be born an opportunity—a necessity—to sell a new American dream to many diverse American consumers. The specialization of American business will arrive to meet the diversification of American consumers.

America in the twenty-first century will be characterized by its differences, not its similarities. America in the twenty-first century will be a mosaic of different ethnic groups and cultures that no longer view assimilation as their American dream.

GLOBAL COMPETITIVENESS: FIVE STEPS TO FAILURE

Richard J. Stegemeier, Former Chairman, President, and Chief Executive Officer, Unocal Corporation

Delivered at the CEO Night of the Financial Executives Institute, Los Angeles, California, February 20, 1992. Used by permission.

This is a pivotal year for America. We're going to elect a president and a Congress. We're going to see if we can pull out of a deep and painful recession. And we're going to see if the other military superpower— the former Soviet Union—can begin to move toward political freedom and a market economy, or if it will fall into darkness and dictatorship once again.

Because it is a pivotal year for America, I wish we were off to a more promising start. In early January, we watched the president and a group of 18 corporate executives travel to Japan to lobby for more favorable trade relations.

"It ain't fair!" they said.

That's the kind of complaint I hear from my grandchildren when they're squabbling over their toys.

I lived and worked in the Far East for thirteen years. In my view, the Japanese are doing exactly what we've asked them to do—selling us high-quality goods at reasonable prices. The Japanese succeed because they work hard. They are well educated. They are committed to quality. And their government does not burden the productive economy with unreasonable regulations and misguided tax policies. I'm sure it is tempting to bash Japan in an election year, but America is starting to behave like the crybaby of the Western world. Not to be outdone, some Japanese politicians decided to retaliate. American workers are lazy and unproductive, they said. Such comments are totally unrealistic.

American workers—at least those I know in the petroleum industry—are as good as any workers in the world. Remember, it was Americans who put out the hundreds of oil-well fires in war-torn Kuwait. And we did it more quickly and efficiently than anyone dreamed possible.

Americans can do the job. I don't doubt it for a minute. We're intelligent, hard-working, and ambitious.

KEYS TO PROFITABILITY IN THE 1990s

Stephen Friedman, Senior Chairman, Limited Partner, Goldman, Sachs & Co.

Delivered to the Securities Industry Association 1993 Trends Conference, April 14, 1993. Used by permission.

Ninety percent-plus of a business is the quality of the people and culture. No doubt, we can spend loads of time figuring out where our business is going, but if we do not have the right team, it won't get us anywhere. A strong culture attracts and breeds good people. Maintaining and nourishing a strong culture is, foremost, the job of the firm's leadership. At Goldman Sachs, we try to defend a tight core of immutable principles from generation to generation:

1. The client comes first.
2. An emphasis on team work.
3. We consider our most valuable assets our people, our capital, and our reputation. If any one of these three is lost, our reputation would be the most difficult to recover.

This tight core of absolutes gives us a point of reference. It makes us comfortable when we address those aspects of the business that must change to keep up with the times. The old adage, "If it ain't broke, don't fix it," leads to complacency and can put us behind the innovation curve. So we ask: "What makes sense under the circumstances?" What businesses are we really in? The answers are not necessarily tied to the past. I will elaborate on this point later when I talk about "Big Ideas."

There are three central issues regarding people in our firm: getting them, keeping them, and helping them improve. We invest heavily in recruiting. We dedicate our key people to it, for both M.B.A.s and lateral hires. Our investment in people is time-consuming and costly. But the cost of turnover, and the cost of having the wrong people, is even higher. We value our people, and we invest in them through training, mentoring, and motivation programs, and through continuing education.

CORPORATE STRATEGIES IN A GLOBAL ECONOMY

Robert J. Eaton, Chairman and Chief Executive Officer, Chrysler Corporation

Delivered to the Greater Detroit Area Chamber of Commerce 1993 Mackinac Conference, Mackinac Island, Michigan, June 4, 1993. Used by permission.

Reasonable men and women can agree on the most thorny issues if they check their ideologies at the door. I've seen it happen. It can even happen when it comes to environmental issues. Europe's environmental problems are far worse in some areas than ours because of its size and population density, and the Greens are as militant as you can get on this issue. But somehow, reasonable and practical compromises get made.

Again, in this country, we seem to go to an "either/or" option right off the bat. You can either have jobs or a clean environment. Pick one! It takes forever to get to the rational middle position. And sometimes we never do.

The fact is, if you're a businessman looking for a place to locate a new facility, you're not afraid of a state that wants to protect its air, its water, its land, and the health of its people. That won't scare you away. It's more likely to *attract* you, in fact. What scares you away is *zealotry*. What sends you to another state is the fear that you're going to be treated as a *target* instead of a potential taxpayer, neighbor, and employer.

STICKING TO YOUR KNITTING: THE INCREASED TREND TOWARD OUTSOURCING

Joe Neubauer, Chairman and CEO, ARA Services, Inc.

Delivered to the Rotary Club of Los Angeles, June 4, 1993. Used by permission.

Since the turn of the century, market share and internal hierarchies were the twin pillars of corporate doctrine. The conventional wisdom driving decision-making could be summed up by two words: control and dominance. For most of the last hundred years, the giants of American industry have used those words as a mantra—creating a corporate culture in the process.

Integration was the name of the game. From the steelworks of my home state in Pennsylvania, to colossal computer corporations, to the four-wheeled legacy of Henry Ford, extending the scope of the enterprise—making it broader and deeper in its range of activities—was the defining corporate mission.

So what was the "company"? In the early days, the company was everything. Some companies fed you, others clothed you, some even housed you. "I owe my soul to the company store" was more than the melancholy refrain of Tennessee Ernie Ford's classic, "Sixteen Tons." It was a way of thinking throughout many of America's basic industries. For many years the culture of the corporation was the culture of the community. Life wound tight around the work place. Whether its soul was a textile mill or an oil rig, a silver mine or an assembly line, dotting the landscape of twentieth-century America was the company town. And ironically, blue collar, white collar—it made no difference—both were the colors of the company man.

SECURING THE AFRICAN-AMERICAN FUTURE: A CHALLENGE FOR TODAY AND TOMORROW

Virgis Colbert, Senior Vice President, Operations, Miller Brewing Company

Delivered to the Omega Psi Phi Fraternity Anniversary, Milwaukee, Wisconsin, November 13, 1992. Used by permission.

I would like to take a few moments to share some personal thoughts on how we can secure the African-American future. However, success will come only if each of us rises to the challenges that face us.

African-American communities today are going through an extremely difficult period of adjustment to a rapidly changing local, national, and global economy. Our people are regularly assaulted by social and economic factors that make it difficult to finish school, to build strong families, or to simply survive. These factors are especially severe in our urban areas, where most African-Americans reside, and are especially acute for many blacks here in Milwaukee.

My perspective on these issues has been formed from observations during my travels across the country, from my volunteer work with community-based organizations, and from my own experience as an African-American male.

While the black middle class has admittedly doubled over the past quarter century, the social, economic, and occupational opportunities of most blacks have worsened. We not only continue to lag behind whites in these categories, but even more disturbing is the expanding gulf between the have's and the have-not's in our black community.

As an eternal optimist, I believe that organizations like Omega Psi Phi Fraternity, with its coalition of motivated, strong and dedicated African-American males will be key in helping black Americans overcome the social and economic barriers in positive and productive ways. After all, what African-American citizens *need today* are expanding opportunity structures, assistance in making positive life decisions, greater access to successful role models, and social and economic support. Omega Psi Phi's creed: "Scholarship, Perseverance, and Uplift" is indeed what African-Americans *need*.

COMPONENTS OF SUCCESS: QUALITY CONTROL, INVESTMENT IN HUMAN RESOURCES, AND APPLIED TECHNOLOGY

Richard M. Rosenberg, Chairman and Chief Executive Officer, BankAmerica Corporation

Delivered to the Executive Club of Chicago, May 21, 1993. Used by permission.

Change may be constant, but I believe successful companies in the twenty-first century—which, for all intents and purposes is already here—will operate against three fundamental components of success:

1. A strict adherence to quality control
2. Strategic investment in human resources
3. Efficient and productive application of technology

Of these three components, quality control may be the most visible and carry the potential for the greatest returns, but only because it may be the by-product of strategic investment in human resources and the efficient and productive application of technology.

John Young, recently retired CEO of Hewlett-Packard, pointed out a startling statistic: Studies have shown that one-quarter to one-third of the time and resources at large companies today are spent *fixing* problems, that is, remedying situations that never should have occurred in the first place. This represents time and resources spent undoing things that could otherwise have been focused on customer service, product innovation, or employee development. It represents—simply—waste.

Obviously, a fundamental goal of successful companies should be to drive out that type of waste, which is why quality control—preventing the problem in the first place—is the key component for successful companies.

U.S. INVESTMENT IN THE NEW SOUTH AFRICA

Patrick J. Ward, Chairman, President, and Chief Executive Officer, Caltex Petroleum Corporation

Delivered to the National Foreign Trade Foundation Council Conference, New York, New York, September 27, 1993. Used by permission.

As business executives, we seek all the relevant facts about the market before forming important decisions. Likely rates of return, statistics on economic growth, production, distribution, and marketing are all important. We also want to know the background of potential business partners, the business culture, and the preferences of our customers. But there is a level of information that transcends factual data. That level of perception relates to the confidence we have in the times in which we live. It has to do with our sense of whether the tide of our fortunes is ebbing or is on the rise.

The existence of a process for change and accommodation suggests that South Africa's tide is rising. The struggle by no means is over. Violence still is a serious problem. Nevertheless, a goal has been set, and the widespread acceptance of that goal is a strong driver for a positive eventual conclusion.

As the political situation improves and basic agreements are reached on a constitution, the economic situation should also improve. As called for by Mr. Mandela, the removal of all remaining international sanctions would be greatly helpful. The focus of the country also needs to shift to the further improvement of the economy in order to meet rising expectations.

To sum up, I believe there are many reasons to conclude that the gains from investing in South Africa will outweigh the risks.

Finally, in all our concern about politics, about economic facts, about expectations, we shouldn't forget the individuals involved. An American company, when it invests in South Africa—with its philosophy, values, and skills—also makes its own special contribution to the economic and social health of that country and to its people.

THE ROLE OF BUSINESS IN EDUCATION

Les Alberthal, Chairman of the Board, President, and Chief Executive Officer, Electronic Data Systems (EDS) Corporation

Delivered to the Dallas Rotary Club, Dallas, Texas, March 10, 1993. Used by permission.

The word "employee" is derived from the Latin word *implicare*, which means "to engage." Now, to me, that means not only to employ, but to stimulate, to win over or attract, to draw into, to involve. That's what we try to do with *all* our employees: to attract them, to stimulate them, to involve them.

Let me reemphasize that word *all—all* of our employees, including (and especially) top-level managers.

You know, conventional thinking is that managers, after they've attained a certain level, don't need development anymore. However, many companies have discovered that even their top managers are not prepared to deal with today's changing business environment. Why? Because they simply never got the right training. So, now, companies—either in-house or via consultants—are conducting learning sessions that include top-level executives, along with middle-level and first-line managers, whom the company has identified as having high potential. And what are they learning to do in these sessions? They're learning to manage—and take advantage of—change.

This just *has* to be done. The best executives of the future will be dealing in a much different environment. They won't be able simply to give orders as they used to. Teams and flattened organization are going to create an entirely new set of behavior patterns, attitudes, and methods of communication. Employees are going to have to understand such things as international competition, organizational versatility, and how to structure international teams and alliances, and yet still *understand* and *accept* accountability.

This strategy, of course, involves the key process of *continuous education* for everyone.

PROGRESS THROUGH INNOVATION: YOU CAN'T HAVE ONE WITHOUT THE OTHER

Robert G. McVicker, Senior Vice President, Technology Group and Kraft Food Ingredients, Kraft Foods, Inc.

Delivered to the 1992 Leaders of the Future Engineering Conference, Pennsylvania State University, University Park, Pennsylvania, April 3, 1992. Used by permission.

Why is innovation so critical to the success of countries, and even to the future of humanity? Because it's the raw material for the creation of wealth; everything else is just reshuffling and redistribution of what we already have. Just as a lever dramatically increases the amount of force you can exert, so does innovation raise productivity, spur economic growth and increase wealth. In a world where everything has its price, technological innovation—though it's not without its costs—is still the closest thing there is to an economic free lunch.

And I'm not just talking about recent innovations like the automobile, the telephone, or the computer. The ancient Greeks gave us the lever, wedge, pulley, and gear. (In fact, sometime in the first century, Hero of Alexandria even invented a coin-operated vending machine to dispense holy water!) In the Middle Ages came the horseshoe and stirrup, which revolutionized transportation and warfare, as well as the chimney, which facilitated home cooking and allowed us to get presents from Santa Claus. Islamic society gave us paper. And the Chinese invented matches, the umbrella, and the toothbrush.

My point is that many of what now seem to us to be the most mundane contraptions actually had a profound effect on human progress. The wealth, comforts, and living standards we enjoy today are built upon thousands of years of innovations, many of which are now so common that it's hard to think that there was a time when they didn't exist. But every generation makes its contributions, just as you will make yours.

THE BREAKDOWN OF THE MONOPOLY OF THE BAR CARD: THE GAME IS OVER

William A. Brewer III, Bickel & Brewer

Delivered to the American Bar Association Annual Meeting, Washington, D.C., August 10, 1992. Used by permission.

The suggestion was put forth in a newspaper article last year that to solve the problem of oversupply of attorneys, the government should pay lawyers $500,000 each to turn in their bar cards. It was proposed as sort of a "farm subsidy" program, whereby the government would pay lawyers *not* to practice law. So instead of say, wheat, the uncultivated crop in the fallow north forty would be litigation. The suggestion was only *slightly* tongue in cheek.

Of course, farm subsidies are used to *keep prices high*.

Oddly enough, what the lawyer bashers have overlooked is that the current oversupply is having some very positive effects; among these are increased *competition* and *efficiency*. Although these are not typically words used to describe lawyers or those in the legal profession, maybe they should be. And that, I might add, is perhaps a more radical idea than paying lawyers not to be lawyers—that is, increasing competition and efficiency in our profession.

Having inherited and protected a business with numerous barriers to entry and restrictions on competition, lawyers have for years enjoyed a monopoly. As every monopolist knows, the ability to achieve monopoly profits is dependent upon the ability to restrict competition. To restrict competition, the players themselves create the rules of the game, which limit admission or entry, by enacting rules of conduct and arcane rules of procedure.

The point is—like it or not—the lawyer glut is one of the significant factors changing the face of the legal profession today. Clearly, we are experiencing a time of dramatic change. It's a buyer's market for legal services, and the oversupply of lawyers is the main catalyst for change. To be sure, billing abuses have provoked outrage over the way some law firms conduct business. Public and media scrutiny of the law firm business has never been greater. Clients are paying increased attention to the quality and cost of legal services, because they have an obligation to do so. And all this portends a shift in the balance of power between clients and law firms.

POLITICS, TECHNOLOGY, AND ECONOMIC GROWTH: THE FREEDOM TO INNOVATE

Richard J. Mahoney, Former Chairman and Chief Executive Officer, Monsanto Company

Delivered to the Council on Foreign Relations—Corporate Section, New York, May 26, 1993. Used by permission.

As a country, we have been living off our national capital, when we should be living off of our national income. Instead of creating a national climate in which business and industry can flourish, and a national climate in which we foster innovation and new technology, we are increasingly allowing others to manage the climate of the global marketplace, while we attempt to micro-manage the weather.

Peter Drucker, in his new book, *Post-Capitalist Society*, notes that the economic performance of both Japan and Germany in the past forty years teaches the same lesson. For most of that time, both countries focused on the economic climate, emphasizing long-term growth, the ability to adapt quickly to change, and competitiveness. Only when they attempted to control the economic weather did they lose momentum.

In the past year or so, we have heard that, to address the problem of America's momentum, we need to undertake what's been called the "third rail" of American politics: a national industrial policy. Even *Business Week* got into the act by calling for what amounted to an industrial policy, but recognizing it needed to be called something else—like a national "growth" or competitiveness policy.

Some define industrial policy as a complete makeover of American business into something resembling the Japanese *keiretsu*—the groupings of companies that dominate the Japanese economy. This American version of Japan, Inc. would require both closer cooperation between competitors—allowed and encouraged by law—and closer cooperation between government and business. Such a policy would have to overcome both American history and tradition, not to mention antitrust law.

PUBLISHING FOR THE INDIVIDUAL: ALTERNATIVES TO TRADITIONAL TEXTBOOKS

Joseph L. Dionne, Chairman and Chief Executive Officer, McGraw-Hill, Inc.

Delivered to the American Association of Publishers (College Division), Washington, D.C., May 13, 1992. Used by permission.

Like many businesses that developed during the Industrial Revolution, we publishers have long been locked into an "assembly line" approach. We would select a manuscript that we felt was worth wider distribution. We would tell the printer how many books we wanted to print, the kind of binding desired, the number of colors needed, and so on. Then the printer would educate us on the costs involved.

By the time the type was set, the plates made, the sheets fed and cut, the pages bound, and the books distributed, assembly-line publishing became a fairly expensive proposition.

This was especially true in textbook publishing. As anyone here can attest, creating a textbook for a national market forces every publisher to take advantage of economies of scale. Rather than a book covering a limited range of interests, a publisher includes virtually every aspect of the topic. The more aspects, the greater appeal in the marketplace. Besides, it's a competitive necessity; everybody else is doing it! Which is how a textbook publisher comes up with the sort of hefty tome that typifies today's textbook market.

Please don't misunderstand: I believe there will always be a place for the traditional textbook. It is efficient. It is often economical. It is even convenient in many cases.

But for many courses and many situations, it is the wrong approach. One thing I'm certain of: Very few of today's core-course textbooks are actually read from cover to cover.

So in a sense the printing press has come full circle: from a "freedom fighter" for knowledge in the fifteenth century to an information "tyrant" in the late twentieth century.

This is one of the realities we've had to confront at McGraw-Hill as we've tried to better serve the needs of our customers. In the old days, we would have tried to make a better textbook.

Today, the marketplace—our customers—is forcing us to reinvent the textbook.

FLASH: THE SKY IS NOT FALLING! A CALL FOR BALANCE

Earnst W. Deavenport, Jr., President, Eastman Chemical Company

Delivered to the Downtown Rotary Club, Knoxville, Tennessee, June 30, 1992. Used by permission.

I am well aware that we in the chemical industry have a poor public image when it comes to the environment. Some players in the industry made some bad mistakes in the past, and history has a habit of following you around.

But a lot of things have changed.

Technology, especially. Eastman's operating procedures and monitoring systems are state-of-the-art. In 1991, we spent almost $200 million on environmental protection and improvements. That's 5 percent of sales; as a percentage, that's more than any other major chemical company. And we've become more environmentally sensitive. We're the energy behind a recycling effort like nothing else in the country.

Several years ago, Eastman and Waste Management teamed up to build a Recycling Center in Kingsport to provide the entire Northeast Tennessee-Southwest Virginia region with a place to recycle glass, aluminum, paper, and plastics. It's been a huge success. In fact, last year, the Recycling Center received a national award from Keep America Beautiful. It's the first industry-community project of its kind in the country.

We're making progress in other areas as well. Our new waste water treatment facility is a good example. It's built off the ground on concrete pillars so inspectors can walk underneath to check for leaks. Innovative stuff.

We're making good progress. That's why I take exception when I hear that the threat of appearing on an EPA toxic list is an incentive for manufacturing plants in Tennessee to "clean up." To paraphrase President Eisenhower: "Hitting someone over the head isn't leadership. That's assault."

CHARTING A LEADERSHIP COURSE FOR MANAGEMENT

John Lynch, Chairman and CEO, Towers Perrin

Delivered at Town Hall, Los Angeles, January 13, 1993. Used by permission.

There's been a lot of talk about quality in recent years, and we're all familiar with the buzz words. Companies have tried various kinds of quality programs, and while some have succeeded, many have failed. Why? Because they approached quality as a separate, stand-alone activity.

To really create and sustain quality, it must become part of the culture and fabric of an organization, not just another mandate from the CEO or a program of the month. Employees must understand and accept the need for quality improvement in everything they do. They must understand how to improve quality, and they must drive the effort. Otherwise, you won't succeed.

That's why Corning Glass involved employees at all levels when it developed its strategy for quality improvement. Corning's goal wasn't to win the Malcolm Baldrige award. It was to win in the marketplace. Motorola is another company that has had great success in this area. It makes quality an integral part of its culture and the way it operates. As a result, Motorola has reduced its defect rate more than 99 percent over the last five years and is still looking for further improvement. It has reduced costs almost $900 million in 1992 alone and over $3 billion cumulatively over a five-year period. Clearly, quality can pay off when it's more than just the management fad of the hour.

Index

Notes

Notes

Notes

Notes

Notes

Notes